Applied Philosophy, Value Theory and Business Ethics

S. R. Bhatt

Originals
(an imprint of Low Price Publications)
Delhi-110052

ISBN 978-81-8454-092-5

Published by
Originals
A-6, Nimri Commercial Centre,
Ashok Vihar Phase-IV, Delhi-110052
Phones: 27302453
e-mail: info@Lppindia.com
url: www.Lppindia.com

Printed at
D K Fine Art Press P Ltd.
Delhi-110052

PRINTED IN INDIA

Contents

Part I **5**
Prologue 7
Paper I
Some Reflections on Applied Philosophy in Indian Context 9
Paper II
Morality, Law, Ecology and Biotechnological Research 35

Part II **47**
Paper I
Philosophy of Education 49
Paper II
Education for Character Development and Career-Making 63
Paper III
Vedic System of Education and Environmentalism 71
Buddhist Economics of Compassion and Communion 83

Part I

PROLOGUE

Philosophy, as a foundation of all knowledge, is essentially practice-oriented. It is both a view of reality and a way of life. It is not just love of wisdom as the etymology of this word suggests, but it is also shaping of life in accordance with the acquired wisdom. It is of course a theoretical enterprise but it is not speculative if it is worthwhile. It has practical applications as theory without practice is lame and futile and conversely practice without theoretical foundation is blind and at random. Practical nature of philosophy was very much emphasized in the Indian tradition. *Dars'ana* (or *Ānvikṣaki*) , the Indian equivalent of philosophy, was recognized as the basis of all modes of knowing and ways of living. The same is true of Greek philosophy as well.

Though philosophy is global in its theoretical formulation, its application has to be local or regional in concrete life-situations and therefore Indian context is predominantly put forth here. There are many works available having western overtones and hence also this shift in emphasis. Since this theme has assumed great importance in contemporary times and many institutions of learning have put it in their syllabus I thought it worthwhile to publish this work which is a collection of my lectures delivered at different places and some of which were published also.

S.R.Bhatt
Former Professor and Chair
Department of Philosophy
University of Delhi
M/P-23, Maurya Enclave, Pitampura
Delhi-110034.
srbhatt39@gmail.com

PAPER I

Some Reflections on Applied Philosophy in Indian Context

Philosophy is both theoretical and applied

Darsána, the Indian equivalent for philosophy, is essentially practice-oriented. It is not just a love of wisdom but also shaping a life in accordance with the acquired wisdom. It is at once both a view and a way of life. It is no doubt a theoretical enterprise but with a definite purpose and a goal to be realized. Therefore, the adjective 'applied' in the expression 'Applied Philosophy' is in a way redundant so far as Indian context is concerned. *Darsána*, which is a preferable usage, has always been practical till the introduction of the western pattern of education. During the last three centuries its practical application has become oblivious and we have gradually become non-cognizant of its inherently practical nature. Lord Lynton in his address to the first session of the Indian Philosophical congress very perceptively remarks, "In the west which delights in definition, Philosophy has been a study; in the East which loves infinity it is a practice." Even in the west now there is a growing realization of its practical nature. It is recognized that philosophy is not an empty or abstract speculative undertaking. Of course there can be pure philosophy in terms of methodology, epistemology, logic, linguistic study etc. but it has also to be applied to the entire life-situation and entire gamut of reality. Philosophy therefore has to be 'Philosophy of ...' in order to be meaningful and significant.

Every system of thought in India has arisen out of the felt need of the age and it has generally served its desired purpose. Most of them have not outlived their utility but either we are not fully aware of it or we have not been able to make use of these systems in planning our life and behavior pattern. In our understanding of these systems there have been some distortions and mutilations due to perverting influence of some vested interests from within and outside.

With the help of two familiar examples this point can be elucidated. The utility of the Yoga system is well-known but it is practiced these days half-heartedly in a populist and a vulgarized way without proper understanding of its fundamentals drawn from the Vedic tradition and systematized in the Sāmkhya system. Not only our information about the Vedic tradition is scant, our exposure to the Sāmkhya system is also truncated as we have been conditioned to confine our information about this system to a later text, viz., Sāmkhya Kārikā of Īśvara Kṛṣṇa. We seldom attend to the Sāmkhya account in the Mahabhārata, the Gītā, the Caraka Samhitā or Ahirbudhnya Samhita and a vast literature prior to the Sāmkhya Kārikā. As a result we have a lopsided view of the system. More or less the same is the fate of other systems.

Like Yoga every system in India has practical orientation and no system can be regarded as complete unless it is applied to concrete life situations. For example, every system begins with an analysis of duhkha or tāpa and the avowed aim of each one is to get rid of it by acquiring knowledge of Reality. This is not just a theoretical exercise. It has a deep and immense practical concern which necessarily calls for *upāya kauśala* i.e. suitable planning, programmes and performance.

The treatment of *upāya* in Buddhism finds its practical application in several treatises like Suvarnaprabhasa Sutram which like the Artha Śāstra of Kautilya provide healthy principles for social, political, economic, moral and religious organization of Society. Like Buddhism, Jainism also has pronounced practical orientation in different *vratas*. The importance of Nyāya system for theory-construction and system-building is well known. The *tantra yuktis* and *nyāyas* of Mīmāmsā provide sound methodological principles some of which have been used in the judicial system of our country. It goes to the credit of the British judges of colonial time that they did recognize the importance of these principles and did care to be informed of them. But the judiciary in the independent India does not seem to pay that attention to them. The multi-volume 'History of Dharma Śāstra' by P.V.Kane has been prompted by this interest of the British judges in the Hindu law. The system of Mīmāmsā further presents a very pertinent account of the principles of management of our corporate as well as individual behavior, both moral and non-moral. They can provide very seminal and fundamental ideas and doctrines even to modern systems of management.

To take another example, Sāmkhya-Yoga, Nyāya-Vaiśeṣika, Pūrva and Uttara Mīmāmsās are not mutually incompatible systems as they have been represented in some text books. All of them are mutually complementary, as has been exemplified in the Caraka Samhitā and Suśruta Samhitā. As Max Muller has pointed out in "Six Systems of Indian philosophy" (P. xvii), " The longer I have studied the various systems, the more have I become impressed with the truth of the view taken by Vijñana Bhikṣu and others that there is behind the variety of the six systems a common fund which may be called the national or popular philosophy, a large *mānasa* lake of philosophical thought and language far away in the distant north and in the distant past, from which each thinker was allowed to draw for his own purposes." Further, these systems are not mere thought constructs. We have their most suitable and conducive application in Āyurveda where all these are employed with success for health and cure in a balanced way keeping in view different dimensions of human personality. Ours is a psycho-physical complex animated and sustained by a spiritual element of consciousness. In *ārogya* we have to cater to all the three. For this Āyurveda accepts the physical analysis of the Vaiśeṣika, the psychical analysis of the Sāmkhya and subsumes both under the spiritual principle of Vedānta. In the works of Caraka and Suśruta we find a very happy symbiosis of all the three.

For writing a history of Indian philosophical thought it is the Caraka Samhitā and not the Sarvadarśanasamgraha which should be our model. B.N.Seal, S.N.Dasgupta, Debi Prasad Chattopadhyaya and a few others have done some remarkable work to point out the practical nature of Indian thought in respect of positive sciences like Physics, Chemistry etc. and Mathematics. We have not incorporated this and similar other material which is now available in writing the History of Indian Philosophy in a fresh way. The lop-sidedness which causes infirmity in the histories written in nineteen thirties still persist in the histories written later on based on the earlier ones.

Another important point to be noted is that foundational character of philosophy has been duly recognized both in the east and in the west. We have regarded it as 'Pradipah sarva vidyānām'. Both theoretically as well as historically it has been regarded as a basic discipline which not only provides methodology and basic principles to all other disciplines but also offers a critique of all disciplines. So it gets involved both at the base and at the apex of all of them. This renders philosophy applied.

Applied Philosophy and Professional Ethics

It is a need of the present times to reflect on the theme of Applied Philosophy and Professional Ethics (Business Ethics) with special reference to Environmental Ethics. It is desirable to do so on the basis of a non-dichotomous, holistic and integral approach to life and Reality, an approach that is characteristic of the classical Indian mind. In the field of philosophy a distinction can be drawn between knowledge as information and knowledge as wisdom, core philosophy and applied philosophy, theory and practice etc. but no incompatibility or cleavage is to be entertained between them. In these pairs the dichotomy is only superficial and not essential. These distinctions are meaningful only at the surface level and for some specific purpose and they need to be resolved in or subsumed under what can be called as deep level thinking.

Symbiosis of Knowledge as Wisdom and Knowledge as Information

In the Indian philosophical tradition we have been told of the distinction between knowledge as wisdom (*vidyā*) and knowledge as information (*avidyā*), particularly in the Īśāvāsyopaniṣad of the Yajurveda. There *avidyā* is not opposite of *vidyā*. It is not nescience or absence of knowledge (and therefore not to be equated with ajñāna) but a knowledge different from the knowledge contained in *vidyā*. *Vidyā* stands for understanding holistic and integral nature of Reality and values to be pursued. It is prescriptive. *Avidyā* describes the means and modalities to realize those norms. A seeker of truth has to know the nature and bounds of both *vidyā* and *avidyā* along with their interrelationship. In the field of ethics we find a symbiosis of the two, as it is prescriptive of the norms and evaluative of the conduct to be judged on the basis of those norms.

PROFESSIONAL ETHICS AND VALUES IN HUMAN LIFE

What is Ethics?

Philosophy is systematic reflection on our lived experiences with a view to be profited from it and one of our most problematic experiences is human behaviour which is indeterminate and unpredictable but concerning which paradoxically constant endeavour is made for determination and regulation. The discipline of ethics is primarily concerned with postulation of norms for good human life and regulation of human conduct in accordance with these norms. Ideally speaking human being is a rational, free and responsible agent. On these presumptions only ethical considerations, ethical theorizing and ethical judgments are undertaken. It is hoped and believed that human conduct can be regulated and be made norm-abiding. This is the objective of the discipline of ethics.

Activity is the law of life and every human being has to act for survival, for sustenance and for enhancement of quality of life. So, human conduct has to be teleological and goal-oriented. In the choice of conduct there is freedom as also regulation of freewill. There is inclusive altenation between freedom and determinism. Rationality as discriminative ability implies freedom to choose but being guided by certain norms. It also implies responsibility for the consequences so generated by ones actions. Freedom to choose means availability of alternatives to opt for that which is good, right and conducive to well-being or to opt for that which is bad, wrong and harmful to well-being. A human being can act in either of the two ways, but he has to be responsible for that action. This determination and choice of alternatives requires norm-prescription but human freedom also implies a scope for both norm-adherence and norm-violation. In this context ethical considerations become meaningful since they tell us about the rules and regulations to be adhered to and prohibitions to be avoided. Values to be pursued and disvalues to be shunned are both equally central to moral considerations. In ethical context values are termed as virtues and this relation between values and virtues should be kept in mind.

Ethics and values

Our awareness of values is always prescriptive. It is different from the descriptive awareness concerning facts. A description can be true or false or doubtful but the logic of prescription has another set of values. A prescription can be good or bad or indifferent. It may be conducive to well-being or harmful or of no effect. A description has to be local with the possibility of universalizability but a prescription has to be global with the need of being applied to local situations. Accordingly the mode of knowing prescription can not be the same as the mode of knowing the description. Of course both are to be grounded in experience but the nature of experience can not be the same. The ideals are conceived in and spring from actual situation but their source is not sense experience.

Another point to be referred to is that norms are posited to be pursued (They are *sādhya* and not *asādhya*). In ideal situation they are to be practiced spontaneously as a matter of habit or by the force of conscience. That is why importance of moral education is accepted as it helps in cultivation of moral will. But more often than not because of moral infirmity built in human nature there is a need of external sanctions, social or political. That is why codes and laws are formulated. But this enforcement from outside is always feeble as moral weakness is ingrained in human nature. That is why there is greater need for moral education and constant vigilance. But it should not be overlooked that values are not to be taught but to be imbibed.

There is always a gap between theory and practice and our endeavour should be to bridge it as far as possible. A moral norm may not be adhered to in its totality or fullness but this does not mean that it should be given up as impracticable or utopian. The distinction between *mahāvrata* and *aṇuvrata* in the Jaina tradition is a good guide in this regard. The mark of an ideal being actually perused is harmony between the inner and outer reality of the agent, between inner feelings and outward behaviour. But this cannot be a fool-proof criterion. Public vigilance helps in norm -following.

Pursuit of professional values both in private and public life

So far as the question of values in private life and public life is concerned, in a holistic and integral approach the public-private divide is not entertained. Values are to be posited and pursued for both the spheres and they are to be sought conjointly. Public life is more demonstrable and loss of values can be detected with greater ease. External sanctions can operate with greater force. But value-pursuit is a collective and corporate endeavour. It is not a single person enterprise. There has to be an all round effort for this. It is physical-mental-spiritual exercise. It is a *yajña* to be performed by the collectivity for the collectivity. This is the message of the Vedas and the Upanisads. We have this cultural heritage available to us, and it is for us to look to it and be benefited by it.

Quest for values, pursuit of values and realization of values have to be holistic and integral exercises. They have to pertain to different dimensions of human constitution, as for example, analyzed in the *pañcakośa* theory of the Taittīrīya Upanishad. Each dimension of human existence is valuable and must be catered to in a balanced and graduated manner. This is the message of this Upaniṣad. There should not be lopsided endeavour, concentrating on one and excluding the rest. Similarly, human existence is situated in multi-layered environment and all layers are to be catered. Human being exists in family, in social and natural surroundings. The *Śāntipaṭha* in the Upaniṣads refers to many such layers. Values pertain to each of these layers. The value-schema should not be regarded as partite or divisible. All values in the schema are intertwined and they are inseperable. No one value can be realized without the rest. There is organic unity in the total reality and this is reflected in value-schema as well. In Classical Indian thought this organic understanding was built-in but now under the impact of western civilization we have neglected it. In our value considerations we have to go back to the classical thought if we are sincere and honest in our enterprise. We have talked a lot about values, particularly in the context of value-oriented education, without caring about the nature of reality given to us in our concrete experience. The reality we talk about is not the lived reality but abstracted reality, rationalized reality and therefore we are far away from concrete reality. It is high time that we shed away our bias against Classical Indian thought, revisit Classical Indian thought and do so in a positive and constructive frame of mind. The contemporary mind is looking for new intuitions, fresh insights and innovative thinking and Classical Indian thought has the potentiality to provide the needed guidelines provided we understand it in its true spirits. The onus of responsibility for this guidance lies on young creative Indian minds and it is hoped that they will prove to be worthy of this task.

NEED FOR ETHICS

Our experience of the empirical world tends to suggest that human beings are the most evolved species in the cosmic process but this does not mean that we are the most favoured ones or valuationally superior most to others. Any anthropocentricism of this sort believing that "Man is the measure of all things" is misplaced. Valuationally every iota of this universe has equal worth. Existential hierarchy does not in any way imply valuational hierarchy. Everything in the universe has both intrinsic and instrumental value. Everything is mutually related and interdependent. Everything has a purpose and therefore is an end-in-itself having intrinsic worth but everything serves a purpose as well and therefore has instrumental value.

So far as human nature is concerned it is as complex as the cosmos. The cosmos is subtle networking of beings, things and events regulated by some universal principle or power. Similarly the human being is also a very sophisticated and fine-tuned networking of psychophysical processes animated by a spiritual principle. Roughly speaking a distinction can be drawn between the psychical and the physical but they are not separable and they closely interact. They are interdependent as well. If we penetrate deep into the very heart of human reality the distinction gets obliterated. The human existence is a miniature organic whole and the cosmos is a whole writ large. Therefore we have not to understand human nature in a fragmented or piecemeal or reductionistic manner.

Human being is self-conscious and reflective person and not a thing or event. We have the capacity to understand ourselves as also others. We draw a distinction between others and ourselves and the distinction is meaningful but it is so only at the surface level of existence. In the ultimate analysis we have to overcome this distinction. Since we are the most evolved and self-conscious beings we have to be most responsible to our own existence as well as to all other existences. We thus carry a universal responsibility. The inanimate things cannot be attributed with any responsibility. The sub-human beings also cannot be entrusted with any responsibility. In fact both these classes of existence have specific and definite functions to perform and they do so naturally and properly unless we human beings tamper with their functioning. So it is we who have to feel our responsibility. In Indian culture our responsibilities are known as *dharmas* and there is a very sophisticated but complicated schema of *dharmas* prescribed. Apart from *dharma*, there are other obligations known as *ṛṇa* and *yajña*. These are determined by our placement in the total cosmic set-up. We have to discharge our obligations as per our placement. These are our roles pertaining to different aspects of our place in the cosmos. These roles are not our choice. They are assigned to us because of our placement. Of course we can change our placement and change our roles, improve our placement and improve our roles, but the role is given to us because of a particular placement only. We have to perform our roles with understanding, with sincerity and with seriousness. This is what the Bhagavadgita teaches in the doctrine of *svadharma*. In order to understand this idea of placement in the total cosmic set-up and assignment of roles as per the placement, it is helpful to use the analogy of an organism. The organism is a unity having a multiplicity of organs. Each organ is situated in the organism at a particular place having a particular role and function. The function of one organ cannot be performed by another organ. Every organ has a distinct and fixed role. But each organ performs its function in communion with the total organism. The outcome of the functioning of each one is not usurped by that one only but is shared by all the organs in communion.

According to the Bhagavadgita a human being is a *puruṣa*, i.e., a rational, free and responsible agent. He is endowed with a capacity to discriminate between right and wrong, good and bad, desirable and undesirable. He has this prerogative but this prerogative imposes responsibilities on him. All his willful actions should be in the form of *puruṣārtha*. He has to perform actions with full knowledge, freedom and responsibility. They should be in the form of ' *artha*', i.e., conducive and leading to well-being. Anything detrimental to well-being is '*anartha*'. They should be in the form of '*iṣṭasādhana*', i.e., means to the realization of good. The good can be material or trans-material, empirical or trans-empirical, this worldly or trans-worldly. According to the Bhagavadgītā there has to be a motive for every willful action and there cannot be any unmotivated action. It does not advocate unmotivated action, which is impossibility. It draws a distinction between motivated and intended action. It prohibits intended action, i.e., an action performed with a desire to get an intended fruit. The term it uses is 'anāsakta karma' and not 'niṣkāma karma'. The latter term which has gained popular currency does not occur in the Bhagavadgītā and its use has caused a lot of confusion. The Bhagavadgītā has repeatedly stated that our actions should be well motivated but we should perform them without being attached to or bound by the consequences. We have control only on the performance of action and we should do it skillfully. We have no control over the consequences and therefore we have to concentrate only on the motive and performance parts of it. The motive has to be in the form of '*artha*' or '*iṣṭa*' leading ultimately to '*loka samgraha*' , i.e., total universal well-being and niḥśreyasa. The author of the Bhagavadgītā, as the Lord of the universe, says that though He has all desires fulfilled still He acts in the mundane world with the motives to set examples for noble conduct, for protecting the good and destroying the evil.

According to the Bhagavadgītā whatever action we perform it should be in the form of a '*yajña*'. No being can remain inactive. Activity is the law of life. But every action inevitably gives rise to its consequences. In the context of human conduct the human being is the primary agent in the performance of action but he is not the sole agent. There are other factors contributing to the effectuation of the action. There is a causal collocation in which human being is one of the factors albeit a dominant one. The consequences of the action are not confined to that human being only. He is not the sole agent and the sole enjoyer. The consequences are experienced by the total cosmos. Anything that happens in one part of the cosmos affects the rest. This is what is meant by saying that we do not have control over the consequences. Once an action is performed it is bound to generate its consequences and they affect the total cosmos directly or indirectly, visibly or invisibly. That is why there is a need to perform action in the form of a '*yajña*' in which the fruits are surrendered for distribution to the totality (Brahmārpaṇa). This is the *karmayoga* of the Bhagavadgītā. This also is the real purport of the doctrine of *karma*, which is a distinguishing and unique feature of Indian thought. This doctrine is at once attributive, retributive and distributive. It attributes agency to the causal collocation in which free, responsible and rational human being is the principal agent. It is retributive in the sense that it stands for a strict causal operation regulating the act and its consequences. Every action has to give rise to its consequences and there is no escape from it. It is distributive in the sense that since the agency belongs to the total causal collocation the consequences also are to be retributed to it in a distributive way. The human being should not try to usurp the total consequences. This is also the purport of the Īśāvāsyopaniṣad which enjoins '*Tena tyaktena bhuñjithāḥ, Mā gṛdhaḥ kasyasviddhanam*". The point is that whatever action is performed it is a collective venture and has consequences for the collectivity. This is the karmic globalization that the doctrine of *karma* stands for.

PROFESSIONAL ETHICS

Human being is a responsible free agent who is rational and discriminative as well. He cannot therefore remain indifferent to the consequences of his conduct. He can act in a way that is good, right and desirable in the sense that it is conducive to general well-being. He can act in a contrary way as well which is harmful and undesirable and therefore should be avoided. This requires regulated conduct and norm-prescription. Though it is not very easy to discern which is desirable and which is not desirable as even the wise people get baffled in this, as the Bhagavadgītā has very rightly pointed out, still in every society and in every age there are enlightened people who provide us with a set of norms and we are expected to follow them.

Because of the presence of free will in a human being there can be norm-abidance as well as norm-violation. Another point to be noted is that it is the prerogative of the human being to have free will and therefore only the human conduct needs regulation. In nature there is inherent uniformity and regularity. Nature abides by '*Ṛta*', an immanent order, but the selfish and ignorant human being tries to temper with it and wants nature to violate its own *nature* resulting in harmful and disastrous repercussions. There is always a constant need to regulate human conduct. This regulation has to be manifold keeping in view the multiple facets of human existence and conative dimensions. The human conduct needs to be regulated not only in relation to other human beings or one's own self but also in relation to the entire cosmos, the social, national and international spheres. So the boundaries of ethics have to be extended to the entire gamut of human conduct. These moral norms are not to be enforced from outside but to be evoked from within. This requires cultivation of a 'good will' or perhaps a 'Holy will' to use Kantian terminology. The ultimate goal of these should be realization of 'niḥśreyasa' referred to above. It should be reiterated that this realization should not be piecemeal, limited or confined to a particular section of the society. It has to be a universal corporate effort and global realization.

Every rational human being has to undertake some profession or the other for survival, for self-fulfillment and for social obligation. It has to be performed for self-expression, self-enhancement and self-realization as an ultimate objective, but its immediate aim is to earn livelihood. In an ideal situation there has to be a balance between the ultimate and the immediate objectives but very often this is overlooked. This calls for professional ethos, regulations and management.

Every profession for its proper and efficacious performance has to depend upon several factors which may be regarded as its guiding principles. There are several criteria on the basis of which the guiding principles can be classified. The most important criterion is the distinction of end-.means-modalities-result (*sādhya-sādhana-itikartavyatā-phala*). Every profession is meant to serve some goal, to realize some purpose and to attain some result. It is the basic requirement of every profession to have clarity about the end for which it is to be pursued. An absence of clarity or confusion about the goal very often results in improper or immoral performance.

The human existence is multi-faceted and multi-relational. Human needs and aspirations are also multiple. All these require a variety of vocations and professions. Every human being cannot undertake all the vocations and perform all the work of every profession. Human capacities are limited though human wants may be unlimited. So human conduct in this regard needs regulation, both intra-professional and inter-professional. Choice of vocation and profession and social guidance in this regard is necessary. Capability, interest, requirements etc. are some of the guiding principles for this. Here also a quadruple distinction among end, means, modalities and result needs to be taken into account to ensure the just, equal and appropriate realization. Intertwined in this is another distinction of knowledge, will, skillful action and distributive enjoyment of the result. Professional ethics has to take into consideration all these components and regulations pertaining to them.

In the cosmic set up there has to be multiplicity of professions depending upon the needs and aspirations and abilities of the human individual. These professions keep on evolving and dissipating as the societies change. On account of human limitations and large number of wants, there is a need for multiplicity of professions. All professions are equally useful and valuable and therefore they should be treated at par, but it is human selfish nature to prioritize them and to put them in a hierarchy. It is a part of professional ethics to respect all professions and to follow the maxim of "Work is Worship". All professions are meant for universal well-being and we have the universal responsibility of upholding their purity and respectability. Unfortunately we seldom care for this.

Every human individual can not perform all the actions and fulfill all the wants by himself/herself, and therefore there has to be choice of vocations. This should depend upon ones capacity, ability, interest and need. The Gītā calls it as *svadharma*. Every one has to mind ones *svadharma*. This is professional ethics. Every profession calls for a code of conduct for its proper performance. The code stands for a set of rules and regulations regarding the two types of quadruples referred to above. There rules and regulations are to be both intra-profession and inter-profession. The Gītā emphasizes both these types of professional ethics. Generally we tend to side track inter-professional ethics and mind only intra-professional ethics. In modern times most of the professions have become inter-professional. For example, medical profession has preventive and curative aspects but it is also intimately related with pharmaceutical, engineering, business, dietary, legal, psychological and many other professions.

There can be as many professional ethics as there are professions. This apart, the number of professions is not fixed. It is determined by the needs and aspirations of human society. Newer professions may come up and older may become a matter of history. Castes and classes may be formed on that basis. Every profession is at once an individual and a group enterprise and therefore the norms and regulations have to deal with both individual as well as group behavior. Their boundaries can be local, regional, national or international.

There can be as many professional ethics as there are professions. Some professional regulations are common to all professions and cut across all of them in spite of their varied nature, modes of functioning, objectives etc. but they also require some separate or distinct set of norms as per their specific requirements.

Every profession therefore has to work out its own norms and regulations keeping in view the ultimate goal of 'niḥśreyasa'. It is a different thing whether it is actually done or not, or done in a proper way or not. It is an ideal though not a utopian one (*sādhya* and not *asādhya* or *dussādhya*). As the proverb goes, "Where there is a will there is a way". Human beings have tremendous potentialities and capabilities. What is required is knowledge, will, devotion and effort. The traditional Indian means to 'mokṣa' are to be understood and reinterpreted in this sense to make them meaningful and significant.

A professional ethics is a management ethics. It pertains to the management of a profession in the sense that it regulates the knowledge, will, skillful performance and distributive enjoyment of results of that profession. In a sense "Ought implies can" and vice-versa and therefore if we can do this management we ought to do it. Proper education is the only way to achieve this. Management through proper education is the sole guiding principle of success in every profession. This education need not be a formal classroom education. It can be imparted in very many ways suiting to that profession and can be devised accordingly. But this much is sure that without management there cannot be proper performance and without education there cannot be proper management.

Legal Ethics

Legal profession pertains to maintenance of law and order and administration of justice in cases of violation of laws and disturbance of order. Here roles of legislature, executive and judiciary, all the three wings of government, are involved. It has many role-players consisting of a body of law makers, civil administrators, and paraphernalia of judiciary, police, jails, and lawyers. Here we take the profession of a lawyer for analysis as an example. The profession of a lawyer is to provide legal assistance to the law court for the sake of maintenance of justice and thereby earn livelihood. The former aspect is primary and the latter secondary. If the secondary assumes the role of the primary, there is violation of professional ethics. The lawyer has to cater to his worldly needs but this should not give way to greed. Even in providing legal assistance for discharge of justice, he should not only know the laws of the land in the best possible manner, he has also to interpret the law and the situation in the given case to safeguard justice. It is not his/her job to prove some one to be guilty of an offense or to be innocent. His job is to arrive or to help arrive at the facts of the case and to establish the truth. And he has to do so keeping the entirety of the situation in mind. If a lawyer thinks that his/her job is only to defend the person he/she is siding with whether that person is guilty or not and this is to be done by any means, fair or foul, there is not only a possibility of miscarriage of justice, it is also a case of violation of professional ethics. In many cases there is miscarriage of justice because the lawyers on both the sides do not care for professional ethics. They wrongly think or believe that their job is to win the case by any means possible. A lawyer may undertake a case for help in adjudication or may not agree to do so. It is his/her sweet will. The accused person has a right to legal defense and it is the duty of the legal system to provide that. But the accused has no right to get exonerated if he/she has really committed the crime. The concerned lawyer can not be held responsible for not shielding him/her. The legal professional ethics is guided by the principles of goodness and rightness. The end has to be good and the means have to be right. The goal has to be pure and so should be the means. The goal should determine the means. Any disparity between the two amounts to violation of professional ethics. The relation between means and end is logical and causal whereas the relation between end and means is justifier-justified. One has to know this interrelationship. Modalities consist in proper, efficient and effective employment of means. This is known in Indian tradition as *upāyakauśala* or *karmakauśala*. This involves procurement of the ingredients of modalities, priority and posterity of their employment, their efficient employment and constant vigilance of the consequences of their employment. This is legal skill which a lawyer has to acquire. Of course legal acumen is innate but skill can be acquired. Finally, the result of action is to be taken into account. It has to be utilized on the basis of distributive justice. It should benefit all those who are involved or affected in that given situation.

It may not be necessary to mention the prevalent violations of legal professional ethics in the society and also the ills and evils of legal system on account of ignorance or non-abidance of this quadruple. We are well familiar with the costly, cumbersome, boring and prolonged litigation procedures which are prohibitive, painful and frightful. The role of money-power and muscle-power, the role of police and other supporting agencies and in fact the roles of all the wings of government, viz. legislature, executive and judiciary, are too well known to us to mention. Any consideration of professional ethics can not be piecemeal. It has to take into account all aspects, facets, dimensions and factors. It is not a matter of simple enumeration of do's and don'ts. Human nature is highly complex and human agencies are very much complicated. Only a holistic and integral approach may be helpful. This analysis is only a brief outline to be elaborated further.

Medical Ethics

We may take up another example of medical ethics in a cursory manner without going into classified details, as it is also very much debated these days. The aim of medical profession is medical-care of public at large for health and hygiene both physical and psychological as body and mind have mutual effects. It has to take into account both the preventive and curative aspects. It has multiform-dimensional as it involves patient-doctor, consumer-provider, state-citizen and such areas of inter-personal relationships. It calls for quality care and general well-being. It demands transparent accountability at all levels, to patients, colleagues, medical councils, state and public at large. Health care has become a team work as for institutionally delivered patient-care service there is team work in hospitals, polyclinics, nursing homes, community health centers, dispensaries, diagnostic centers etc. and team ethics involves ethics for doctors, nurses, para-medical workers, auxiliaries, community workers etc. It has attracted the role of mass media (generally nicknamed as media-trial), and also civil, criminal and consumer protection law courts. We are very well familiar with violations of and deviations from medical ethics. Beginning with pollution in atmosphere, adulterations in eatables and drinkables and use of duplicate and expired medicines, there is rampant commercialization and profiteering. Medical care has become costly and at times unaffordable and prohibitive. Service motto is almost lost. Professional self-restraint is decreasing. There is paucity of effective laws and regulative authorities are becoming weak. There is organ sale and misuse of diagnostic procedures. There is public-private sector divide, with weak public sector and profiteering private sector. There is public subsidy but no public care. Even there are cases of medical graduates joining administrative services. This is another case of either ignorance or non-abidance of the above stated quadruple. The instances can be multiplied. The point to be noted is that medical ethics is multi-pronged. It comprises both the hygiene and health aspects, preventive and curative aspects, individual and community lives, and all the five dimensions of human life as stated in the *pañcakośa* theory of the Upaniṣads.

Enviornmental Ethics

On account of lack of restraints, selfishness and proneness to feed to the greed rather than catering to the needs all due to ignorance there has been all-round pollution of the environment. The human individual and for that matter all living beings are inherently bliss or blissful whatever be the nature and description of bliss. The inanimate world that environs living beings is bliss-yielding. This is one of the implications of the spiritualistic approach to life and reality. In case of the human beings there are five types of environments (kośas) described by the Taittirīyopaniṣad as we have stated earlier. When we talk of environmental ethics we have to take into account all these which though inseparable need to be distinguished for proper and effective management. These five types of environment run parallel and yet they interact affecting one another and their functioning cannot be regulated in isolation from one another. The vital powers affect the functioning of the body. The vital powers in turn are molded by the mental functioning. The functioning of the mind is influenced by the intellect. A holistic and integral view of environmental ethics along with a differential treatment of each type of environment is the proper way of approaching this issue. The Vedic seers are very particular in this regard. They strive for purity of the intellect (*dhī* or *prajñā* or *vijñāna*), mind (*mana*), vitality (*prāṇa*) and physic (*anna*) all together. They prayed for the health of all these environments in their diverse forms and facets. All these are regarded by them as distinct but not separate as they have their source and sustenance in 'That one' named as '*Puruṣa*' or '*Brahman*'. The purity of the physical depends upon the vital, the purity of the vital upon the mental and purity of the mental depends upon the intellectual. All these get purified when they revel in bliss (*ānanda* or *rasa*). Human conduct needs to be regulated in a synthetic-cum-analytic mode to ensure harmonious, balanced and proportionate functioning under all these environments in a smooth and progressive way in the cosmic process.

In modern times we are voicing concern for only the physical environment being oblivious of other ones that are equally important. Because of this lop-sidedness we have not been able to make much headway in protecting the physical environment. We do not much bother for the protection of the other three without which the fourth one also cannot be protected. There cannot be a divisive approach to environment or to the total reality. We have to pay due heed to the Vedic message which is the very foundation of our survival and progress leading to perfection.

Though we should pay equal attention to all types of environment and devise ways and means to regulate our conduct in respect to them and thus may have five different types of environmental ethics, for the present we may concentrate on the physical. Here also voicing environmental concern in seminars, conferences, lectures etc. is not enough. What is needed is creating environmental awareness or consciousness and inculcation of the spirit of responsibility and accountability in our relation with nature. A sustainable development leading to more and more perfection stands in need of environmental stewardship. Environmental stewardship implies a sense of mutual care to be spearheaded by human beings only. If we care for nature, nature will care for us. This is a corollary of the famous dictum, "*Dharmo rakṣati rakṣitaḥ*". What is required is not the attitude of consumerism and reckless use of material resources, domination over and exploitation of nature, but responsible use, equitable distribution and preservation of the splendors of nature (*vasudhā*). The present day ethics and ethical practices are too human-centred to recognize the 'reverse relationship' between nature and human, to posit a relationship of mutuality between human and the rest of the creation. To use another terminology of the Bhagavadgītā, of the Artha śāstra of Kauṭilya etc. the human being has to cultivate the attitude of '*yoga-kṣema*' towards the nature and the rest of the cosmos. Then only we can meet the needs of the present and future generations by a developmental process that is really sustainable and progressive.

The task of an environmental ethics in the context of physical environment is to devise norms to regulate our conduct in respect of nature in all its facets at the individual and institutional levels in local, regional, national and global spheres. There should be a paradigm-shift in our moral code along with widening the scope of ethical considerations to bring in regulation of human conduct not only in relation to other human beings but also between human beings on the one hand and other living beings and inanimate things on the other. There is a need to formulate a charter of environmental conduct and create environmental awareness in human beings through proper and adequate education and through enactment of suitable laws and their strict enforcement by institutional mechanisms both governmental and non-governmental. The eco-syllabus should take into account global ethics, both preventive and curative. It should aim at regulating our conduct in the spheres of earth, water, air, fire and space, the *pañcabhūtas*. It should be kept in mind that the main problem is not the effect of our conduct on the environment but our relationship with the environment. This requires the role of human beings as preserver and protector of environment, accountable as caretaker. It could also be that the human being should approach nature with love, adoration, respect and gratitude, as most of the ancient cultures have enjoined. Their religious regulations though primitive are most advanced from this point of view and need to be taken into account.

The spiritualistic approach implies that the nature needs to be looked upon as our own self, sharing and partaking the same essence and therefore it has to be protected not so much because it is useful as because it has its own inherent worth. In fact every element in the cosmos exists in itself though it also exists for others. The self and not-self are only to be distinguished and not to be separated.

Though all world cultures, religious and spiritual traditions and primitive modes of living present a unifying vision of cosmic existence, the Indian culture has placed special emphasis on this which needs to be reiterated time and again. The 63 Mantras of the *Prithivi súkta* of the Atharva Veda enunciate a theory of eco-spirituality that has perennial relevance and significance. The classical Indian perspective on eco-philosophy is very rich and sublime. Nature has been given the status of mother. Nature and every aspect of nature are regarded as worship-able and adorable. Worship of nature is the keynote of Indian way of life even today. So if the Indian masses offer worship to land and mountains, rivers and seas, plants and trees, birds and animals, it is not an exhibition of primitive animism as some mistaken scholars may tend to believe. It is an expression of our love, regard and reverence to nature that sustains us and provides us nourishment.

Mistakenly human beings think that nature can be conquered and we can have mastery over it. But nature is too mighty to be controlled by tiny humans. Human being is himself a small part of nature in his psychophysical aspects and therefore he has to remain subservient to nature. Nature is kind and merciful, bountiful and benevolent, caring and loving. It has instrumental value for human being. We should understand and appreciate its instrumental worth and make use of it judiciously for our betterment in a selfless way. Nature is usable. This is its *nature*. We have to understand this *nature* of nature. This requires proper understanding of nature through natural sciences and adoption of proper practices towards it through technology. We have to cooperate with nature in order to enable it to cooperate with us. Unfortunately the modern so-called civilized human has not been able to live up to this requirement. In the name of development not only nature has been badly mauled and mutilated resulting in ecological crises, it has also generated problems of intra-generational and inter-generational inequality. The Indian perspective again can be helpful here. The ideals of *asteya* and *aparigraha*, the concepts of *araṇya* (no- conflict) and *pañcavaṭi*, the practices of *vana mahotsava* and vṛkṣāropana etc. are only some of the multiple illustrations of our living in harmony with nature.

While concluding we may only hope for the betterment of human thinking and living in the spirit of spiritual globalization with mutual care and share, love and cooperation. The best ideals of global ethics can be found in our *śāntipaṭhas*, *svastivacanas* and *subhāṣitas* that are available in plenty in our classical thought and in the writings and sayings of sages and saints of our country. The syllabi on eco-philosophy and the code of conduct in eco-ethics should incorporate them.

PAPER II

Morality, Law, Ecology and Biotechnological Research

It is a very important theme for deliberations which is of great contemporary relevance and significance. It is significant area of philosophizing which has stemmed from our present needs and aspirations. To philosophize is to reflect upon our lived experiences. It has to be a systematic reflection. Of course, systematization has its own demands and it may render our thinking a little tough and sophisticated. But if we are clear in our thinking, we can be quite at ease and simple in our communication. We would be doing a sort of philosophical reflection on the theme which is quite vast, multidimensional and having variety of facets. We shall be very brief, and yet we shall try to be clear.

Human being as rational, free and responsible agent

We live in this cosmos which is not static but dynamic process. It is very intricate, fine and subtle interplay of living beings, things and events. In this cosmic process there is a purpose. It seems to be goal-oriented but our finite mind is unable to comprehend what precisely is the purpose of this cosmic process and where this cosmic process is leading to. Quite often we find that our activities are purposive and goal-oriented but our mind is unable to comprehend what precisely is that purpose. In this cosmos though we have a variety of living beings and inanimate things and events, it is the human being who is the most evolved and most developed creature fro that reason she/ he takes the center stage. Human being should be and therefore more responsible. Unfortunately this is not the.case.

A human being, ideally speaking, is a ratiocinative, goal-oriented, free and responsible agent. These are the three properties which a human being is bestowed by the cosmic process. We are ratiocinative in the sense that we have the ability to distinguish between right and wrong, true and false, good and bad etc. We exercise our abilities at times but quite often we do not. Likewise, we are goal- oriented and therefore in our enterprises, in our endeavours, we must be very clear, and knowledgeable as to what should be our goal. In the performance of our action, in the ways of thinking and modes of living unfortunately again we are not so much clear with regard to our purposes. We are responsible beings for whatever action we perform. Every action has to generate its consequences and the consequences must primarily be apportioned to principal agent. We are the principal agent being supported by some ancillary conditions. The Bhagavad Gītā enumerates five conditions for the performance of action and human agent is only one of the five, though the dominating one. Since we are the most evolved, we tend to dominate. Though we are having intrinsic value, we are proud of our intrinsic worth and therefore we tend to think that everything else is instrumental for us. Everything should serve our purpose. Other living beings should serve our purpose. Due to ignorance we forget that others also have intrinsic worth and we can be instrumental for their well-being. Ignorance means improper, inadequate understanding of the nature of reality. It is because of this egoity, we are not responsible for our agency. But we have to act in this universe in a responsible manner.

Need for action and its regulation

We have to act for our sustenance, we have to act for enhancement of our life, for a quality of life but not of our own only, in fact it should be for the entire cosmos. We have to act, we can't remain inactive, but as a ratiocinative agent we must know the consequences of our actions and be responsible for them. In fact the entire moral philosophizing originates from this because morality is concerned with regulation of our activities. Entire moral reflection aims at giving a direction, a desired direction, to our activities and this has been so from time immemorial. It is not that moral philosophizing is a need of present time, it was so right from the start of the cosmic process and if we look back to our hoary past we may learn some very good lessons from our heritage. Our heritage is more than 5000 years old as it is known to us and it is handed down to us as a *paramparā* (tradition). By *paramparā* we mean that we are firmly rooted in our past, by it we stand up in our present and through it we have a vision of the future. We have a long *paramparā* and in our *paramparā* we have been told that human action needs to be always regulated in the sense that choices are given to us. We may choose this alternative or that alternative. That freedom is given to us and we must exercise that freedom but once we exercise a particular freedom and choose a particular course of action we are responsible for that.

In our tradition no strict distinction has been drawn between morality and law in the past. The term that we used conjoining the two is *dharma* but the specific aspect of *dharma* which regulates conduct was also known as nīti and when it was through political intervention it was known as rājadharma or dandanīti. The distinction between morality and law is of western vintage, of Greek inheritance. Any way, if we want to draw a distinction, the distinction could be like this that morality provides internal sanctions for regulation of human conduct whereas law has the external sanctions. But it was always pointed out both in Indian tradition and in western tradition that law of parliament can not make a man moral. External sanctions do work but to a particular extent. The real force belongs to the internal sanctions and therefore there is always a need to season law with morality.

Another very significant distinction was drawn in the tradition to which attention needs to be drawn. A distinction was drawn between 'in- authority' and 'an-authority'. The Śāstra is 'an-authority'. The sanction should come from 'an-authority'. It should be impersonal. 'An-authority' should never be personal because a person is liable to be selfish, liable to be lopsided in thinking, liable to be prejudiced and so many infirmities belong to a person who is finite with narrow vision, with distortions of egoism. Therefore it was emphasized that 'an-authority' should always be impersonal. It could be Śāstra in ancient times. The Dharmaśāstras were there, the nītiśāstras were there. It could be a constitution in the modern times. But an-authority should always be impersonal and it is always desirable that it should be codified. So instead of oral traditions, it should be in written form. In England also constitution was earlier quite oral. But now it is in written form. In India we have a constitution which is 'an-authority' for our conduct. Now this authority should be exercised so that human conduct is regulated and for that we require a person or a body of persons 'in-authority'. To ensure the smooth functioning of 'an-authority' we require 'person in authority'. So the impersonal is now personified. But then with this personification of an authority all ills and evils creep in. We are familiar with the way our legislators function, the way our executives function and unfortunately the way our judiciary functions. In modern times we favour democracy as a mode of political governance. But we are painfully aware of the pitfalls in the functioning of democracy.

It may be pointed that a time has come when we should think beyond democracy. No where in the world democracy has succeeded and therefore there is a need that philosophers should come out with a new paradigm of political governance so that the sanctity of an authority is preserved and the 'persons-in-authority' do not pervert and mutilate an authority. In ancient times we had *purohits*, we had *mantries* to advice the king and at the time coronation the king was required to undertake a pratijñā (vow). In the Mahābhārata we have a very good account of pratijñā, to be taken by a king and in order that king should understand the spirit of a pratijñā, he was given training as a yuvarāja in many disciplines. So we had the checks and balances. Unfortunately we do not have those checks and balances now and therefore there is a need to have morality in law. Earlier we were not bothered about this caption 'morality in law' but now since 'an authority' is endangered by persons 'in authority' , there is a need to reflect on 'morality in law'.

Technology and universal responsibility

We have to act for living, for betterment of our living. Normally we would have acted naturally. But we want ease in our actions. We want smoothness in our actions. We want to accelerate, enhance our capacity to act, and therefore we make a transition from nature to culture. From natural mode of behaviour, we try to adopt the cultural mode of behaviour and the most sophisticated form of culture is technology. Through technology we want to empower us more and more. It is good thing of course. The transition from nature to culture is a welcome change but it has a big proviso and we must be aware of that proviso and that is the technology is usable with care and concern, technology is to be used only for well-being and not for destruction. Technology is the practical application of scientific enterprise and scientific investigations. Through science we try to discover the inner potentialities of nature so that those potentialities can be harnessed and utilized for our well-being. But we forget that our well-being is not that of isolated individual human being. In fact our well being is the same as the cosmic well-being. We are part and parcel of the cosmos .We can not have our well-being apart from the cosmic well being. Lord Buddha in his intuitive realization of the nature of reality has propounded the well known four noble truths and talked of universal interdependence of all phenomena. A teacher of physics these days is familiar with the quantum physics formula of interpenetration. Any thing that happens here has the repercussions in the remotest corner not only of the earth but of the outer space as well. The ozone layer that we are worried about is the consequence of our activities. So this doctrine of universal interdependence 'pratītya samutpāda' was put forth by Lord Buddha centuries ago. The point is that whatever we act whether as an ordinary person or as a scientist or as a technocrat we must be alive to our universal responsibility. By universal we mean the cosmic responsibility and therefore we have to follow the quadruple principle of human responsibility. (a) We must know what is true, good and desirable because we are vivekī, we have the capacity to know. It is different thing whether we cultivate that faculty, we enjoy that capacity, we make use of that capability or we do not and very often we do not. But we have the capacity of knowing what is good and what is not good and when we say good, it is not individual good but is always cosmic good. Real good is the cosmic good, bare individual good is only delusion, it is false understanding. So we must know but we should just not know. (b) Knowledge if it is genuine knowledge must result in intense desire to act in accordance with that knowledge. A scientist may claim to know the reality of the nature but in fact it may be only a pretention. He may not really know the reality. And if he knows the reality then he will encourage only such technological inventions which really lead to good and do not have any evil or harmful consequences. (c) So knowledge must stir in us a good will and when there is a good will, there must be good actions. (d) And if there is an action, then there must be a result of the action and good will alone can give rise to good actions and good results. These are the four principles, on which a meaningful and purposive cosmic process must be based. In Sanskrit terminology we express this as *jñāna, bhāvanā, kriyā* and phala.

Technology for universal well-being

Another quadruple principle which is equally significant is as follows. There are two types of activities. One is instinctive activity which is automatic and the other is the voluntary one. Whenever we undertake voluntary action, we must know why we are doing so. The goal, the *sādhya*, the *lakṣya* for which we should undertake that activity must be known rightly. That goal must be, not just desirable but really desirable in the sense that it must be in the form of cosmic well-being, in the form of *Lokasamgraha*. In order to realize the goal, which is necessarily good, intrinsically good, we have to select the means in accordance with the goal, conducive to the goal and which really leads to the goal. If we take wrong means then we can not reach to the desirable goal. So it is the goal which has to determine the means to be adopted. The *sādhya* should regulate our choice of the *sādhana*. *Sādhana* or the means should not only be appropriate to the ends but should also be available and accessible. We can think of hundreds of means but if these are not available or accessible, it is merely an idle thinking. It is mere utopian thinking. A *sādhya* is not utopia, it is not *asādhya*. It has to be realizable and if it has to be realizable, there must be appropriate and adequate means to realize. So if we are knowledgeable about the goal, if we are knowledgeable about the means, we should also be knowledgeable as to how to make use of these means, the employment of the means, and this means the modalities. Since the universe is very complicated, intricate and phased process, we must know the different phases of the modalities, which phase should come first, which phase should come thereafter. The priorities and posterities, we should know. Then finally we must also know what sort of results will accrue from that particular action. This is the philosophy of management of action advocated in the Gītā. The Gītā is the best manual for philosophizing with regard to the way we should think, the way we should behave. But the Gītā also propounds the philosophy of the management of results of action. The Gītā says among other things that whatever results accrue they are to be renounced to the total cosmos (*Brahmārpaṇa*) So *Brahmārpaṇa* should be the guiding motto for the performance of action. The results are not to be enjoyed exclusively by us but along with others. This is the message of Yajurveda also, the culminating portion of which is Īsāvāsyaopaniṣad . It says 'Tean tyaktena bhuñjithāḥ', we have to enjoy the fruits but along with others. It is a philosophy of cooperation; it is a philosophy of mutual caring and sharing. This should be our guiding spirit.

Technology and use of natural resources

Again with regard to technology we get guidance from the Gītā . A technology is employment of natural resources, of course, to be added by human resources but basically technology is concerned with employment of natural resources. And natural resources are depletable. The Gītā therefore always enjoins to approach the nature with *yoga* and *kṣema*. These are the two cardinals principles advocated in the Gītā. Kṣema means whatever resources are available in nature, we should try to protect and not deplete them. We can recycle them. We can look for alternate resources. Nature is so much permissible that it allows recycling of its resources. The Sāmkhya system, for example, tells us about Prakṛti giving rise to vikṛtis and the latter merging back in the former. It is a cycle. So recycling is permissible in nature. Not only recycling is permissible but acceleration is also permissible. The nature has capacity to expand its power, its mode of functioning. *Yoga* means to augment and therefore we have different instruments invented by technology to augment our capacity to make use of natural resources. *Yoga* and *kṣema* therefore are concerned with the production through technology. But after the production, when we have the produced, again the Gītā tells that we must be guided by the principles of *asteya* and *aparigraha*. These are two important foundations along with three others which we know as *vratas*. Anything which belongs to others, if we deprive them from their legitimate use, it is *steya*. Therefore whatever we have, is to be shared in distributive way. This we call as intra-generational justice. We talk of the 'haves' and 'have-nots', we talk of the underdeveloped and developed countries, we talk of the north-south divide, these are all the cases of *steya*. The Gītā says that we should see to it that this sort of malpractices come to an end and we exercise *asteya*. But the Gītā is not just concerned with present generation. The Gītā, and our entire Indian tradition, is also concerned with the future generations and so we talk of inter- generational justice in the form of *aparigraha*. We should not use natural resources in such a way that nothing is left for the posterity. We have a right to live, we have a right for quality of life but so also our sons and our grandsons and therefore we have to care for them. We are familiar with a story of an old person sowing a mango seed and someone asking why are you sowing the mango seed because you can not reap the fruit of that. He replies that my sons and grandsons will reap the fruits. *Aparigraha* stands for the tradition of intergenerational justice. *Parigraha* means just pocketing the material goods whether we need them or not and not to care for the future generations. *Aparigraha* means to care for the future generations.

Unfortunately we have not given proper attention to both scientific investigations and technological inventions in terms of their benevolent roles. We do raise our concerns and concerns are voiced in different fora. Right from politician to lay persons, intellectuals to common men, every one is voicing concern but none cares for consciousness. We are not conscious of the root cause of malady. If we read the classical literature, we find that our ancestors were conscious of science policy and regulations of technological inventions. We are not conscious of that in modern times and consequence is different ecological problems that we are facing. Again with regard to these issues we are guided only by the analysis of symptoms. We are not concerned with the root causes. We only say there is global warming or there is hole in ozone layer. But why in the ultimate analysis we have these faulty tools of scientific discoveries and technological inventions we are not really concerned with that. In Yajurveda there is a famous hymn "*Tanme manaḥ Śivasamkalpamastu*", i.e., let my mind be guided by noble and pure intentions. Buddha has also said that if we have *kuśala citta*, our *karma* will be *kuśala*. If we have *akuśala citta*, our *karma* will definitely be *akuśala*. It is the mind which guides us to act this way or that way. This is the opening verse of Dhammapada, a popular Buddhist text. All problems arise from our mind .Vedic ṛṣi says that nature is *ritambharā*. Nature is law abiding, nature is orderly. But who disturbs the order in nature, nature itself does not disturb it. It is we human beings who disturb the order in the nature. We are responsible for that. Unfortunately we do not feel responsible for that. And therefore we have to look within. This is real deep ecology. All the environmental issues arise because our thinking has gone astray. Our mind has become impure and our vital breaths have become infirm. We feel only concerned of the issues because we only raise voices and we do not have the consciousness. If we have real concern, we have to cultivate that consciousness that if anything is impure in my neighbourhood it also affects me. So we should not clean only our own houses and throw all the dirt into our neighbour's houses or to the neighboring streets or to neighboring countries. America thinks that they can throw their nuclear wastes in some far off places in ocean. But it definitely affects America. They do not care for the environment of others but forget that they also have to suffer the consequences. The point therefore is that let there be genuine philosophical reflections. The philosophical reflections are with regard to the concrete issues, not with the abstract things. Philosophy is not abstract brooding. Gone are the days when under impact of western philosophy we were doing 'arm chair thinking' in the name of philosophy. Philosophy is theoretical and therefore it must have practical implications. Darśana is not mere speculative. It has to deal with life. In the past we had philosophizing in the battle field as in the Gītā. We had philosophizing in libraries. We had philosophizing in the laboratories as Caraka and Suśurta did. Philosophy can be done any where and every where if we are alive to our problematic issues in our experiences and undertake systematic reflections on those experiences.

Part II

PAPER I

Philosophy of Education

It has been said about the Hegelian philosophy that it died of being misunderstood. The same has been the case with general philosophy as well. So much has it been misconceived, mistrusted and misused that the word 'philosophy' is more often than not used contemptuously to brand anything that is vague, confusing and abstruse. To a great extent the so-called philosophers and the teachers of philosophy are responsible for this plight of philosophy. Therefore, before we embark upon our avowed task of establishing the correlation between philosophy and education, we shall do well to see the exact nature and function of philosophy, education and philosophy of education.

What is Philoshopy?

Etymologically, philosophy means love of wisdom but functionally it means both the seeking of wisdom (process) and the wisdom sought (product). This wisdom, it must be made clear, is in no way mere abstract ratiocination. It really means practical orientation and vision (for use in life) based on pure knowledge. Philosophy, thus, stands both for the theoretical knowledge of the nature of reality and nature of life and its conditions, and the practical (applied) knowledge of the principles of conduct for the guidance of life. It is a systematic reflection over the entire reality with a view to fathom its mysterious potentialities. Human life is the most important facet of the reality and therefore it is one of the most important tasks of philosophy to solve the riddles of human life and existence.

In twentieth century under the impact of empiricism and positivism an attempt was made by some philosophers to restrict the scope and function of philosophy to mere linguistic analysis. Undoubtedly such an analysis has its own importance to clear the rubbish from the path of philosophical thinking but that is not the end-all and be-all of philosophy. That is just the preliminary task. Philosophy has to do something deeper and more serious. It has to address itself to the imminent problems facing the humankind, failing which it would cease to be the 'Queen' of all the disciplines. It is redeeming to note that in twenty first century there is a welcome shift in philosophizing and philosophy has become applied as well.

Against this background we can formulate three important tasks of philosophy viz,

(i) to study the nature and phenomenology of our knowledge, and to formulate the norms and criteria of its sources, validity and truth.

(ii) to ascertain, in the light and by the means of the instruments and equipment so developed, the nature of the reality - within (human life), without (external world) and above (supra-mundane Reality).

(iii) and, finally, in the light and on the basis of the enlightenment so gathered, to develop and formulate, for life's guidance, the goals or values and the means and modalities to realize the same.

What is Education?

Education is a deliberate conscious process which consists in a modification of the natural development of human. Human is imperfect by nature. His life is a process of development which tends towards something which is more perfect. This results in the modification of his behaviour pattern. In order that this modification may not fall short of its goal it must be well engineered. This presupposes an adequate formulation of beliefs and aspiration of human existence which, in other words, are called as aims or objectives of education.

Education, moreover, is a medium through which the society transmits its heritage of past experiences and their modifications, system of values and the modes or skill of acquiring the values. Thus, all education is a means for the betterment of human life. It is the fruitful utilization of the knowledge attained by the humankind for the enhancement of human existence.

Philosophy and Education

Every philosopher, if he is to make his philosophy of any worth, must determine what his philosophizing implies for the process of education, because to know is to be (i.e. knowledge for the sake of being) and in order *to be* education is the only means which is proper and adequate. History of humankind testifies the fact that all the great educators were also great philosophers, and their philosophical views were inevitably reflected in their educational schemes.

Since education is an instrument for the betterment of life, all educational questions in their ultimate analysis rest on the philosophy of life. Although not very many of the modern educationists attempt for a precise formulation of their philosophy of life, none can afford to miss it. As it has been said, there can be no alternative between philosophy and no philosophy but only between a good philosophy and a bad philosophy. If the dependence of education on philosophy is that inevitable then why to neglect it; why not to admit it from the front instead of pushing it in from the back?

The modern estrangement between philosophy and education has been unfortunate for both. Such of those modern educationists who tend to rely on empirical sciences at the despise of philosophy need only to be reminded of what ancient thinkers had said that true education is practicable only by a true philosopher, or what they had warned that the belief that human beings may continue to educate without concerning themselves with the subtle problems of philosophy means a failure to understand the precise nature of education. Similarly present day 'philosophy-scholars', who betray the restricted view of the sphere of philosophy, should also be told that Plato and Hume, Russell and Whitehead, Husserl and Wittgenstein etc. from whom they have derived inspiration, did not regard education as a study unworthy of philosophical consideration.

What can Philosophy Contribute to Education?

If the general philosophy is a systematic reflection over the entire life to understand its nature then educational philosophy is also a systematic reflection comprehending the phenomenon of education in its entirety. Every system of education has to base itself on certain ends and policies, and it is the business of philosophy to provide these ends and policies to education. The framing-up and selection of the educational ends and policies presuppose value-considerations and value-judgements. The discipline of education because of its positive nature cannot make normative decisions. Hence is the need of a philosophical framework.

All the major issues of education are, at bottom, philosophical. We cannot examine the existing educational ideals and policies, or suggest new ones, without considering such general philosophical problems as the nature of the good life to which the education should lead; of human himself, because it is human we are educating; of society because education is a social process; and of the ultimate structure of reality which all knowledge seeks to penetrate.

Philosophy is helpful to education in four important ways;

(i) in providing theories of human, society and the world;

(ii) in suggesting the ends and means of the system of education;

(iii) in examining the rationality of our educational ideals, their consistency with other ideals and in ruling out the part played in them by wishful or unexamined thinking; in testing the logic of our concepts and their adequacy in explaining the facts they seek to explain, and in demonstrating the inconsistencies among our theories and indicating the precise range of the theories that are left when the inconsistencies are removed.

(iv) and, in evolving a suitable system of educational planning and administration and a teaching-learning strategy for effective and efficacious educational process.

Philosophical Foundation of Education

Every system of education must have its footing on the solid basis of a systematic reflection about the nature of reality (*sat*), knowledge (*cit*) and values (*ānanda*). Of the three philosophical foundations of education, viz., ontological (pertaining to *sat*), epistemic (pertaining to *cit*) and axiological (pertaining to *ānanda*), it is the epistemic which is the most fundamental and therefore the foremost in importance. This is because, through reality has existential priority, it is knowledge which has noetic priority. That is, in order that there has to be knowledge at all, there must be a prior being of Reality. But in the noetic process knowledge reveals Reality and thus acquires priority. Therefore, from a human point of view the approach to Reality is only through knowledge and there is no passage from Reality to knowledge. As regards value it rather constitutes the very culmination of the process of existence and knowledge, and thus comes at the end.

Facets of the Noetic Basis of Education

Knowledge plays a fundamental role in the sphere of education. It is the very stock, so to say, in the trade of education. And that is why a theory of knowledge is quite basic to any theory of education. The epistemic inquiry helps to evaluate the educational thoughts and practices, develops them and thus enables us to use them as instruments of human progress. One of the important functions of education is the acquisition and imparting of knowledge, but before we undertake this teaching-learning process, it is desirable to know the nature and sources of knowledge itself so as to get an insight into the complexities and intra-connections of its diverse forms and facets. This would not only help us in maintaining proportion and perspective in curriculum but would also enable us to avoid the superficial and get at the essential. Further, education is a purposive activity, devoted to the development of individual's personality. Its direction and shape are determined by human beliefs, aspirations, aims and ideals, which in turn are based on and moulded by knowledge. Education thus is determined in structure, contents, range etc. by the varied forms of knowledge and their hierarchical inter-relations, and therefore no theory, and for that matter the practice also, of education can be complete and enduring if it is devoid of its noetic foundation. We may now discuss in brief some of the broad areas where epistemology provides a basis to education.

Knowledge, Values and Education

Philosophy, and epistemology for that matter, is concerned, among other things, with the problem of value. This is because philosophy attempts to study Reality keeping human being in the focus. The quest after values, and the attainment thereof, constitute the very core of human life. There is an innate necessity for man, caused by his finitude and imperfection, to participate in the process of value-realization. Now all questions about values (not of values) are basically epistemological. For example, what is the nature and the sources of values? What kind of existence do they have? How can they be acquired? And such are the questions which presuppose the capacity of human mind to know values. All these questions are equally relevant to education. For example, if it is said that it is only by effort that one can know and realize a value, this is just the same as to say that experiences which educate are fundamental to value-realization. A way of looking at value epistemologically necessarily needs to look to educative activities as means for their realization.

From the above, it is quite evident that the process of value-realization is basically an educational one. There is an educational dimension indigenous to axiology and reciprocally there is a necessary connection between educational objectives and value-seeking. The process of education tends to refer to a set of values or ideals embodied and expressed in the objectives for which knowledge is imparted. That is way the questions as to what is human and what he aspires for, are the unavoidable preamble to any kind of education, formal or informal.

Nature of Knowledge and Education

The problem of nature of knowledge has occasioned a severe controversy in the field of epistemology. Different schools of thought, starting with different metaphysical assumptions have taken different positions and have offered different answers for this. These various epistemic approaches have greatly influenced and moulded the thought and practice of education. They have reflected themselves in similar corresponding shades in the sphere of education. For example, if knowing is identified with doing, as a pragmatist or instrumentalist would do, its natural consequence in the field of education would be a stress upon activity methods, like projects, experiments, problem-solving etc. The only genuine knowledge would be knowledge-in-action. The possession of a body of certified knowledge would be at a discount. The past heritage may be doubted and discarded. The contemplative and meditative sides of education, quiet enjoyment of literary and artistic pursuits etc., would be neglected and emphasis would be laid on knowledge by acquaintance.

Instead, like a realist, if knowing is regarded as representing something which is there outside to be known, then education would be regarded as a medium of revealing the outer reality to the knower. Learning would be regarded as true and effective if pupil's impressions correspond to outer reality. The learner would be regarded as a passive instrument, having an empty mind, a tabula rasa, as Locke would put it, when he would start the process of knowing. Through curriculum only that knowledge would be imparted which was already known to the teacher and the text-book writer. All new inventions would tend to be regarded as mere discoveries. More emphasis would be laid on natural sciences and knowledge of the external world. Religion, spirituality and disciplines based on introspection etc. would be put to disuse. Knowledge by description would not be discarded, but, on the contrary, established traditions would be banked upon.

As an idealist emphasis would be laid on the constructive activity of the mind out of what is given in immediate experience. Knowledge would not be regarded as about existence but as existence itself (*Brahmavid bhavati brahma*). The pupil would be regarded as 'in the process of becoming' and education as the means to the fullest efflorescence of the potentialities of human lying hidden in him. Education would be a constant training of body, will and mind. It would consist of not mere study of books etc. but of active participation in, personal identification with and real embodiment of what is known. In the learning process self-activity, introspection, meditation etc. will acquire prominence. As against the traditional formal and naturalistic education of the realist there would be greater freedom for imaginative insight. Spiritual education would occupy a place of honour in the curriculum.

Further, if by knowledge we mean only that which is stated either orally or in writing then such a view would certainly put a premium upon verbal examinations. If by knowledge we mean that which is useful in adjustment, then, like the pragmatist, practical efficiency and experiments would be relied upon. If by knowledge we mean inner experience which is ineffable, as a mystic or intuitionist would contend, then the consequences of such a view would be that written examinations would be put at a discount.

Now a little reflection on the metaphysical assumptions with which these schools start would make it clear that they do not use the word 'knowing' in one and the same sense, and hence is the diversity in their positions. The pragmatist uses the word 'knowing' in the sense of that activity, mental or physical, which helps the man in his struggle for existence with a hostile environment. The realist, however, uses the word 'knowing' in the sense of the mental process which enables a man to mirror the external reality with which he had to get himself adjusted for the advancement of life. An idealist, on the other hand, uses the world 'knowing' in an altogether different sense. Since he does not believe in any outer reality friendly or otherwise, for him all knowing is 'self-knowledge' only and it consists in being aware of one's own 'Being'. This analysis clearly suggests that there is no antagonism in the diverse positions adopted by these schools and they can be regarded as complementary. They refer to different phases of life and reality and therefore in a particular context each one is true. This conclusion would certainly have a tremendous effect in the field of education since the educators are very often led to think that these schools are quite incompatible and educational implications of one school can never be compatible with the educational implications of the remaining schools. Such a fallacy of exclusiveness can be brought to the notice of the educationists only through the analysis of the epistemological positions of the so-called conflicting schools.

Source of Knowledge and Education

With regard to the sources of genuine knowledge, again, there has been no unanimity among the philosophers. Different thinkers, having different background and assumptions, have emphasized different sources like sense-perception, reason, intuition, revelation, authority, etc. These differences resulting in characteristic positions have reflected themselves heavily in the planning of educational activities and programmes. For example, an empiricist who discards all a-priori knowledge and accepts only a-posteriori, would place an exclusive weightage on science and would fawn upon philosophy and cognate rational disciplines. A rationalist, on the contrary, would bank upon a-priori knowledge. He would discard all empirical studies as superfluous and would harp upon purely theoretical and intellectual pursuits. A pragmatist, again, would go to another direction and accept only those disciplines which are based on immediate experience and which are helpful to the individual in promoting and furthering his life and existence. He would emphasize vocational and practical education.

Here, again, a calm and serious reflection would help us to realize the fact that diverse are the facets of reality and hence diverse are the ways to know it. Consequently none of the recognized sources of knowledge is false or complete. In the all-enveloping gamut of knowledge each finds its adequate place and hence none should be discarded. Such a synthetic vision would have a tremendous impact in the sphere of education and would help to remove all false dichotomies.

Validation of Knowledge and Education

One of the major tasks of education is to acquaint the pupil with the true criterion of knowledge. That education cannot be regarded of any worth and sense which does not enable a person to discern what is right, good and useful. No education can be perfect and complete if it merely concerns itself with bare acquisition of knowledge without inculcating the ability to test its validity in concrete life situations. The optimum development of personality, which has been the recognized aim of education, requires the cultivation of a reasonably adequate pattern of judgement, and this can be provided only by imparting the definite criterion of meaning and truth. This is what is called the education for critical faculty. This has been the nature of education in ancient India.

Different criteria for truth have been advocated in different schools of thought. At the philosophical level preference for one or other of the criterion has been usually made in different schools under different metaphysical and epistemological assumptions. But in actual practice most of us are likely to use all the criteria usually proposed, with the emphasize shifting from one context to another. In daily affairs in which our beliefs are concerned with the objects, qualities and relations that can be perceived we tend to accept the criterion of correspondence. On the other hand, when we are concerned with formal problems, dealing with conceptual relations, we tend to rely on the coherence test of truth. Instead, if we are concerned about the truth or desirability of complicated practical judgements, socio-political arrangements, we tend to use a pragmatist test judging the consequences of action in terms of the more or less well-established norms or values of a culture. In the field of education such a position would result in the synthesis of the triple tests of truth. This would widen the scope of curricula.

Knowledge and Curriculum

Knowledge plays a tremendously important role in the framing up of the curriculum and the scheme of school organization. The curriculum being the only avenue of approach to knowledge it behoves us to understand the nature of knowledge. Knowledge is the very essence or the soul of the curriculum. A curriculum design or pattern is distinguished by the way in which it embodies knowledge. Therefore before any framing up of curriculum can proceed, the curriculum framer must fully acquaint him not only with the nature, sources and criteria of knowledge but also with the hierarchical organization and priorities or disciplines with regard to their teaching through the curriculum.

In the light of the above analysis of the problem pertaining to this area, we can examine the various traditional forms of curricula and by an evaluation of their points of strength and weaknesses we may evolve another form which may suit the growing needs of the country. The problem of explosion of knowledge can also be solved by discerning the essential from the superficial. Here we may put forth the following criterion for the discernment, viz., and 'what would be desirable for every human as a human to know?' and the answer to this may provide us with the guideline for the formulation of curriculum.

Knowledge and Teaching-Learning Strategy

Since the aim of all education is to impart knowledge successfully, the success of the teaching-learning strategy lies in properly knocking at the door of knowledge. The curriculum is the store, as it were, in which all knowledge is locked up. The teaching-learning dynamics is the key to open up the lock and to lay open the stored knowledge. This can be made possible only when the key is suitable to its purpose. This not only brings teaching-learning strategy nearer to knowledge, but also makes that process dependent on knowledge.

Different approaches to the nature of knowing and learning and their relationship would tend to make a difference in the nature of teaching-learning process. For example, a pragmatist would want an active school, an active pupil and an activity-oriented programme. The function of a teacher would be not to impart theoretical knowledge, but to organize, select and direct experiences so that the participation in the activities may bring the maximum knowledge to the pupil. The interest of the pupil would be heavily relied on and it will be the responsibility of the teacher to stimulate, arouse and direct the interest of the pupil. The pupils would not be asked to be engaged in fruitless memorization but will be taught to think through the problems. A realist, on the contrary, would stress on the attainment of the knowledge of precise relationships between two facts, events or objects. Learning would be regarded as conformity to what is outwardly true. The mind of the pupil would be repeatedly impressed with the nature of the external things. Drill, memorization of the well-established information, careful observation and constant checking of facts etc., will be some of the means of moulding the understanding to conform to what is objectively so. An idealist, on the other hand, would insist that education must conform to the supreme ideal of humankind viz., fellowship with the Ultimate Reality. Here the teacher would be given a place of position and importance. Interest, effort, discipline, self-study, self-education, freedom of will etc., will be the main features of learning process. The idealist would not make the pupil a devotee of any one particular method, but rather would like him to be a creator of method.

The above consideration would lead us to one important conclusion, viz., knowledge is the end and the teaching-learning process is the means to acquire it. No means can be successful in the acquisition of its avowed end unless it is in conformity to its end. So it is the nature of knowledge which would determine, or from which would follow, the shape of teaching-learning strategy.

In India at present we are experimenting with regard to the suitable and congenial form of teaching-learning strategy. But unless we are clear with regard to the nature of knowledge we have to impart and also with regard to the curriculum which we have to evolve and frame, it would be quite futile and pointless to labour in experimenting upon the precise form of teaching-learning strategy. As a matter of fact such a thing would naturally come by way of consequence or corollary of the curriculum.

The upshot of the foregoing considerations is that from every angle of the educational problems there comes a demand for a noetic-basis of education. The art of education will never attain complete clearness in itself without this basis.

PAPER II

Education for Character Development and Career-Making

What is education?

Education is a deliberate process of modification in the natural growth and development of human being and the surroundings. It ensures accelerated process of development in human life in right rhythm. It is therefore a means for betterment and enhancement of life, a means to bring about quality of life with the help of social and natural surroundings. Education undoubtedly is a major force to go ahead in life in a meaningful way. In so far as education is a conscious and planned effort to organize life, education and life are intimately correlated.

Education, moreover, is a medium through which the society transmits its heritage of past experiences and modifications, systems of values and the modes and skills of acquiring them.

Role of knowledge in education

Knowledge plays a very fundamental role in the scheme of education. Aim of all education is to impart knowledge effectively and thereby generate 'life-skills'. In Indian context the generic term "*Vidyā*" has been and can be used to comprise information, instruction, skill, training, knowledge and wisdom or realization.

Human being has an inherent need to know what is 'within' and what is 'around' in the surroundings. This helps in betterment of life by making best use of that knowledge. In this sense 'knowledge is power' and it helps in empowerment of the individual. Knowledge prepares successful life-entrepreneurs among human beings who can carve a niche for themselves. A person who possesses adequate knowledge can soar to great heights of success in all walks of life. He/she can develop the capacity and confidence to take on the challenges of life which do come in the way. Knowledge generates the feeling of self-worth, self-respect and self-confidence, and independent existence which is the authentic existence. Through this he/she can command respect from others as well. In this sense knowledge is an elevating and enhancing force.

Education for Personality Development

A robust, vibrant and holistic education ensures all-round development of an individual. It provides opportunities for fullest possible efflorescence of inherent potentialities and enhances capabilities to realize this. Personality development should mean character development, fullest possible manifestation of natural traits implicit in our being. Of course it does involve transformation of natural propensities, and this is the goal of culture, but this should not be unnatural or anti-nature. Culture is non-natural but not anti-natural. The Vedic seers addressed humans as "Amrtasya putras", which implies that we are no doubt finite but we are born with infinite potentialities and we can infinitize our finitude. All individuals are innately born with some dormant personal traits unique to themselves based on which they can be distinguished. These traits are amenable to endless transformation. Education helps in their enhancement. It is a sure means of development of body, enrichment of mind, maturity of emotions, sharpening of intellect and illumination of spirit. Thus it is a process of physical, vital, mental or emotional, intellectual and spiritual growth. The Vedic seers exhorted humans by saying, "*Manurbhava janayā daivyam janam*". That is, "Be a person and cultivate noble qualities in life". For this realization role of education was highlighted. In Indian tradition two accounts of value or goal of education are available. One is, "*Sā vidyā yā vimuktaye*" and the other is, " *Sā vidyā yā arthakari*". Both these are complimentary as education has to serve both the purposes. On the one hand it should be ennobling and liberating from imperfections-cognitive, conative and affective, and thus leading to character formation, on the other hand it should also be enabling for good quality of living. Thus, personality development as character-development and career-making are the twin purposes of education.

By introducing better living, both in terms of character - development and career-making, education creates interest to go ahead in life with greater strides. It thus provides meaning to life and also a sense of fulfillment and satisfaction. Therefore it can be said that education is most important thing other than peace of mind. In the course of life favorable or adverse circumstances come unexpectedly and there may be ups and downs in life. It is only right type of education that can enable us to bear and endure and carry us through. In this sense education is a life-prolonging force.

Education for Living and Livelihood

Education is an important tool not only for survival, but also for quality of life in the competitive world. By cultivating life-skills for vocational choice it is a preparation for life, a living with dignity and joy, with economic self-sufficiency and material comforts, with mental happiness and spiritual satisfaction. It opens up glittering careers, booming career options and attractive career advancement by creating a knowledge hub. Education as knowledge serves as a motive force for vocational choice, as "success vitamin" or "ladder to success" by generating competitive excellence and thus leads to brighter tomorrow. Career planning is a process that should go on through out life as we evolve and grow with our experiences. This is so because the occupational world is dynamic and expanding, job market is volatile, newer opportunities become available and therefore there is demand for professional development in the work-situation. As T.S.Eliot remarked, "It is in fact a part of the function of education to help escape not from our own time-for we are bound by that-but from the intellectual and emotional limitations of our time." Thus education is a liberating force from poverty and deprivation, stagnation and decadence.

Career planning should also be a process in accordance with ones nature and inherent potentialities. It has to keep in view the goal of career-making, the means and the modalities involved. Without adequate awareness or knowledge of these any attempt in career-making is hazardous and at random. There has to be vocational planning. The goal must be desirable and in conformity with ones nature. The means must be in accordance with and conducive to the goal and the employment of modalities has to be skillful. The end, means and modalities constitute an organic unity in keeping with our psycho-physical make-up.

Education is a Hall-mark of Civil Society

Education is a unique gift to and a prerogative of human being. It alone distinguishes a human being from lower animals. It is thus 'human-making", makes a human being worth the name. Right type of education provides for democratic thinking and living. It is character-building and results in refinement of conduct. It generates enlightened and responsible citizens. A value-oriented education transforms human life from savage to civilized state of existence. It broads the vision and enlarges the heart ant thus paves way for mutual caring and sharing, by making us live together in peace and harmony. It is thus an ennobling force. It elevates from ignorance, superstitions, false beliefs and moral infirmity. It is compared to precious wealth that can not be stolen, an ornament a human being can adorn. This thus provides respectability to human being.

There are multiple benefits of education and therefore every human being should try to get best possible education and it is the responsibility of parents and society to provide the congenial atmosphere and opportunities to every human being to get proper and adequate education so that he/she could march ahead in life with full satisfaction and adequate realization.

Education for Character Development

In contemporary times the humanity is acutely facing the crisis of loss of character, a sort of value-entropy and value-negativism. It is not that this is a recent phenomenon. In every period and in every society this was felt but the magnitude is much alarming in the present age. Resulting in all-round destructive behaviour and the irony of the situation is that it has become natural to our mode of living. The problem is how to ensure the needed character development, how to overcome the chasm between knowledge of values and realization of values. There is explosion of knowledge but correspondingly there is no enhancement of life, a life worthy of human being.

Character development is basically a relational notion. It stands for cultivation of certain qualities which are which are necessary to make human life worth living. These qualities may be in relation to one own self and in relation to others. The generic term "self-realization" stands for qualities in relation to ones own self. A human being in order to be called a "person" in the true sense of the term has to develop discriminative awareness (*viveka*), must have the capacity to exercise free will (*icchā-svātantrya, svarāt*) and must be responsible for ones conduct (*bhoktā*). The other facet of quality cultivation is in relation to other human beings, all living beings and nature. Two virtues "*maitri*" and "*karuṇā*" can envelop all these qualities. In Indian culture and in classical system of education these qualities were highlighted. It was also emphasized that for cultivation or realization of these qualities family, society and state all the three were responsible.

In modern times we have not only forgotten these noble qualities but we have also, so to say, disowned our responsibility. The consequence is that there are multiple problems facing human race. Unfortunately we are alive of the problems but we tend to attend the symptoms only and do not bother to go to the roots of the problems. The roots are not confined to the sphere of educational scenario but are spread all-round. One has to go outside the educational arena also to the environments of family, neighbourhood, caste or clan, work place, market place, society, nation and world at large .In fact the modern technological developments have relegated the educational set up to the backdrop, parental mediation has declined and a new type of group influence mostly unhealthy and perverting has arisen as television and other mass media have acquired overpowering influence on human mind. Nevertheless, the role of education need not be minimized. Education can be geared to manage the media and re-mould the human character, which is the need of the times. We live in a media dominated age, an age in which the principles, ideals, symbols and images that give direction to our life and provide our sense of 'being' are largely presented by the media through varied and vast means of array of agencies. Through proper education we can make use of this medium to speak to us with messages that are ennobling and which may tell us what we are, what we have to be, what we have to do how we have to live, and thus supplement class room influences. It should be noted and emphasized that character development is a natural-cum-social process rooted in human individual but shaped by all types of environment. A holistic and integral perspective and an organic approach to life and reality is the real solution of this malady and there is no other way out of this labyrinth. We live in a world of co-existence and interdependence, of mutuality and reciprocity with the 'other' and therefore respect for the 'other', mutual care and share, universal responsibility and not just demands for rights can surely rectify the situation. Given the requisite knowledge, will and courage it is not impossible though it is difficult and requires universal all-round systematic and planned endeavour. It is hoped that sooner or later saner sense will prevail upon humanity. This has been the message of seers and sages all over the world at all times.

PAPER III

Vedic System of Education and Enviornmentalism

The present paper aims at expounding the core of the Vedic system of education in relation to environment which has universal value and perennial appeal. The main objective of education is to impart the liberating knowledge which enables a human being to attain the sumum bonum of life.[1] This alone provides a meaning and value to human existence and makes life worth living. This distinguishes human existence from the rest of the existences, both animate and inanimate. The Vedic system of education has the capability to meet these requirements and to fulfil our aspirations and it is flexible enough to get suitably modified and transformed according to the needs and projections of the 21st century.

Before undertaking the exposition of the Vedic system of education it will be helpful to first explain the meaning and nature of value-orientation in education as it is the essence of Vedic education. As stated earlier the quest after values and the attainment of values constitute the very core of human existence. There is an innate necessity in a human being to participate in the process of value-realisation. This is caused by his/her imperfection and finitude and awareness thereof. That is why, consciously or unconsciously value-concepts, value-discriminations and value-judgements feature prominently in his/her life. Let us also not forget that the process of value-realisation is basically educational and it tends to refer to a set of values embodied and expressed in the objectives for which education is imparted. Since education must have some defininte objectives if it has to be meaningful, effective and of any worth, it is quite natural to ask, 'What is it that education thrives to accomplish?' A consideration of this question necessitates a sort of value-thinking, for it is value-decisions alone which can provide valid and adequate objectives. Value considerations are so widely pervading the sphere of education that all educational decisions presuppose or involve value-decisions. For example, what is to be taught (ends and objectives involved in the curricula), how is to be taught (methods), whom is it to be taught (fitness, motivation and interest of the pupil), how to evaluate the performance of the pupil etc. are the issues which demand value-considerations. In all educational activities value-involvement is inevitable. The more teacher or educator is made aware of the realm of values so much more he/she is able to open the vision, understanding and the perspective on the life of the person being taught. The more immature the pupil is the more responsible the teacher has to be. A too narrow or biased valuational perception on the part of the teacher is a serious danger to the pupil. It is therefore highly necessary that the educator is first educated valuationally. As such value-education is necessary not only for the pupil but also for the teacher or educator.[2]

Once we have grasped the fact that the nature of human being and therefore of education is such as to require him/her to participate in the fulness of life, to be receptive of the significant and to be open to whatever has meaning and value, the question arises as to what is valuable in life and in the world. In other words, what should we appreciate and imbibe so as to be a person in the full sense of the term. The question in short is how we can discern the values of human life and existence. In order to get a right answer, it may be profitable to look at the Vedic thought in this regard.

According to the Vedic thought the entire cosmos is teleological, purposive and goal-oriented. There is a built-in telos, or *Ṛta*, which sustains, controls and directs the entire world process.[3] The total reality is one *Puruṣa* (a perfect Being), says the Ṛgveda.[4] We are all offsprings of that *Purusa*, though we may not be aware of this fact. We are therefore under obligation (ṛṇa) to realise the Puruṣahood inherent in us through proper and meaningful endeavour (*puruṣārtha*). The Vedas tell us that we are the progenies of the immortal *Puruṣa* (*amṛtasya putrāḥ*)[5] and we are required to strive for the restoration of our prestine purity, perfection and immortality.[6] Our present state of imperfection and finitude is not our original nature. It is an imposition, a covering and a bondage to be removed. Our goal should be to get rid of it and to be back to our original nature which consists in perfection and freedom from wants and suffering.

According to the Vedas education is the basic means to attain perfection and freedom. And there is no other way. A real education is that which helps us in realising this state.[7] So the ultimate goal of Vedic education is man-making. It should turn out a *puruṣa*, a genuine human being (*Manurbhava janayā daivyam janam*).[8] From this goal all aims and objectives of education should follow as corollaries. A true education must help in enabling us to live a quality life, a life which is worth living, through a balanced, harmonious and all-round development of the individual, the society and the entire cosmos. This is what is meant by value-oriented education in the Vedic context, both in the sense of 'values in education' and 'values of education'.

The Vedic system of value-oriented education is based on the vision of the Reality as apprehended by the Vedic seers. They find an abiding and enduring place for values in the very heart of the reality. The description of Reality as '*Saccidānanda*' implies that all existence (*sat*) and knowledge (*cit*) culminate in bliss (*ānanda*) which is the ultimate value.[9] In the human beings because of their finitude and imperfection the values are only partially reflected. But every individual is potentially perfect and has the capacity to be perfect. So the ultimate aim of every individual should be the fullest efflorecence of the value essence lying hidden or dormant in him/her.[10] It should be made clear that this realisation is not a mere utopian dream. The values are realisable and they are to be gradually inculcated through proper endeavour. That is why they are called *Puruṣārthas*. They are the objectives of human efforts. But this is not possible until and unless all impediments in the process of growth and development are removed. Here comes the role of education. The quest after perfection is a collective endeavour in-volving all and encompassing all. The Vedic hymns like "*Samgacchadhvam samvadadhvam sam vo manānsi jānatām*", ", "*Sahanāvavatu saha nau bhunaktu, saha vīiryam karavāvahai*"[11] etc. are replete with these ideas. So the planning and pursuit of perfection is not an individual enterprise in isolation from the so-ciety and the rest of fellow beings or even the cosmos. The Vedas therefore emphasise communitarian and participatory living in an organicismic mode. Though the *puruṣārthas* possess a sort of unity for the sake of easy understanding and puruit, they can be classified under two heads, viz., *preyas* and *śreyas*.[12] *Preyas* pertains to material well-being while *śreyas* consists in spiritual realisation. Though these two refer to two different orders of existence, there is no incompatibility between the two. There is no schism between the two orders of being and hence no bifurcation and incompatibility between matter and spirit. *Preyas* provides the material base while *śreyas* constitutes the spiritual summit of the same process of value-realisation. There has been a tendency in the West to uphold a false dichotomy between science and spirituality but this has not been accepted in the Indian thought. Likewise it has been fallacious on their part to make a distinction between values of matter and values of spirit and treat them as separate pursuits. The two are in fact complementary, the former providing a base to the latter.

Education is a preparation for life. But life is not mere live-lihood. Similarly life is not mere catering to the demands of either matter or spirit, body or soul.. There is no exclusive 'either-or' between them. No human being is merely a professional being whether an ordinary worker or a scientist or an engineer or a doctor or an industrialist etc. Likewise no human being is a recluse or samnyasin The Vedic thought adopts a holistic approach to life and reality and therefore calls for the education of the whole human being and not just get confined to some aspects only. Hence the fulness of education consists in and must comprise all the facets of existence-physical, vital, mental, intellectual and spiritual. In the Taittiriya Upanisad we have an illuminating account of these five dimensions of human personality. It is known as the theory of *pañcakośa*.[13] In their togetherness they constitute the total person-ality. Following the Vedic view in the modern times Swami Vivekananda, Mahatma Gandhi, Tagore, Sri Aurobindo etc. have all emphasised that a true and adequate education must aim at the total person.

It can be argued that the above account and analysis may be theoretically sound but the question is how to put it into practice. Its practical viability can be demonstrated by providing a blueprint of the education for the values of matter, for the physical dimension (*annamaya kośa*) which is the first and the foundational dimension. A similar blueprint can be prepared for the values pertaining to the other dimensions as well.

Matter gets manifested in human body-mind complex, in material goods human being makes use of and in the sorrounding environment in which he/she lives. All the three are organically correlated and provide a base to our worldly existence. The Upaniṣads declare matter to be the basic reality. The Taittirīya Upanisad says, "*Annam vai Brahma* "[14] Matter has an intrinsic existence as well as an instrumental worth for human beings. We have to care for both these aspects ignoring none at the cost of the other. But we have to be very careful in making instrumental use of matter. We have to learn to take due cognisance of the worth or utility of nature which is the cosmic manifestation of matter. We must be benefitted fully from it by making its judicious use and not be diseased by misusing it.[15]

This consideration leads us to the delineation on the values of matter. We shall again delimit our account to the gross form of the human being. Broadly speaking there are two kinds of values of matter in its gross form. One is health and the other is hygiene. One of the basic and primary aims of education should be to develop a healthy person with a sound mind and for this it is a prerequisite to teach the practice of the values of health and hygiene. Recognition of health and hygiene, both individual and public is the hallmark of a civilised society. They are essential for the socio-economic as also for the total development. A balanced consideration of the values of matter has to take into account all the levels of existence-individual, social and cosmic-and all the forms of matter which are five-fold according to Indian thinking, viz., earth, water, fire, air and space (both inner and outer). Matter is manifold and mutative and we have to understand it properly and make use of it judiciously.

The psycho-physical health of an individual is the first and foremost requirement. It is a truism to say that only in a healthy body healthy mind resides and where there is psycho-physical health there is spiritual solace. For this, apart from cleanliness of the body and the external surroundings, purity of eatables and drinkables is also necessary. And therefore what should be their intake and in what quality, quantity and modality should be the subject matter of physical education right from the very beginning of the educational process. If the body gets nutritious food and clean environment, it will have immunity from disease and a body having ease is conducive to the development of mind and sustenance of spirit. The Indian seers have always insisted on primacy of health as it is the basis of the realisation of all dharmas. For this they have prescribed many instrumental values like *śauca, saṁyama* etc.[16] In the educational curricula there must be inclusion of the contents pertaining to positive health and hygiene. This should include information about food and nutrition and also about eco-ethics. Education for positive health and hygiene is replete in Vedic hymns, and apart from copious references to environmental planning and management through divine help there is a specific *Sūkta* called *Bhūmisūkta* or *pṛthivisūkta* in the Atharva Veda in which the sage Atharvan advocates environmental stewardship and eco-sensitisation. This *Sūkta* must form a part of any meaningful syllabus on eco-philosophy.

Health is an internal value whereas hygiene is an external one. Production of good quality unadulterated material goods, maintenance of purity of natural environment, a pollution free and clean surrounding, cleanliness of body, clothes, home, town and other surroundings etc. all come under hygiene. Health is primarily an individual value but hygiene is a social and collective value in which every individual has to participate and contribute to every child has to be taught to cultivate the civic sense of health and hygiene both inside and outside. To get to details, taking bath daily, cutting of nails, brushing the teeth, cleaning the clothes, dusting of the house, eating and drinking judiciously etc. are a few instances. Likewise construction of well-ventilated and sunny houses, sanitation of lavatories and tiolets, cleanliness of kitchen and living rooms in the house and of lanes, roads, parks and other public places all these should be the basic and important subject matter of education at different levels in different forms. Dignity of labour and *śramadāna* should be taught to every pupil in the spirit of the *Karmayoga* of the Gita. "Work is worship", this slogan is not just for professing but it should be put to practice. Every one should be taught to do some work of cleanliness and planting or nourshing plants and trees as a matter of daily routine. It should be like a *svadharma* or *nitya karma*. For cleanliness there should be no dependence on others as far as possible. It should be practised both at individual and social levels. It should be obligatory that not only one should be clean oneself but should also help and make others clean. In our consideration of hygiene we cannot stop at this level only. In the modern nuclear and supersonic age we have to be very careful about purity of the entire cosmos both in its microscopic and macroscopic forms and in any meaningful education cultivation of environmental value-sensibility must be an essential part. Negligence of this has already affected seriously our present living endangering our health and hygiene and unless we pay due heed to it, there is every possibility of extinction of life on our planet. The sooner we realise this the better it is for our well-being and survival. In this context it is very pertinent to draw our attention to the famous '*Sāntipāṭha*' of the Veda in which purity of the total cosmos is aspired for and we are enjoined to strive for its realisation and preservation. The '*Sāntipāṭha*' in the Yajurveda expresses our intense longing as follows

"May there be peace (and purity) in the outer and the inner space, on the earth, in the waters, in the vegetable kingdom both eatable and non-eatable, in the entire cosmos, in the entire reality, everywhere and at all times. Let there be peace and peace alone. May every one attain and experience peace. May peace and peace and peace alone prevail."[17]

Indian sages and seers visualised the need and significance of ecological balance for the welfare of human beings as well as for all living beings and inanimate things. They realised the essential unity of the cosmos and realised the organic character of the inter-relationship of its parts. They advocated an integrated approach to developing balance, harmony and mutuality so that there could be no exploitation of nature by human beings who are corruptible. They insisted that need rather than greed should be the guiding principle in our relationship with nature. They devised traditions, customs and rituals with this objective and attached religious sanc-tity and sanctions to the need for the purity of nature. They introduced festivals and celebrations with the idea of inculcation of such thoughts, beliefs and practices by interspersing deep religious convictions. They invented myths and legends to bring home the significance of nature and its purity. They opined that nature in its infinite forms and countless modes is nothing but a manifestation of the Almighty God. This intrinsic divinity of nature led them to salute and worship all the five basic forms of matter known as *pañcabhūtas*. For example they beseeched, "That divinity which is in fire, which is in water, which pervades the entire universe, which is in eatable vegetation and in non-eatable vegetation we respect-fully salute it." In addition to this positive reverence which finds manifestation in tree-worship, animal worship and in various other forms of nature worship, they negatively inculcated a deep rooted belief in the form of aceruance of papa (sin) and adharma (evil) in case any violence is done to nature by us. There was also a prescription of *prāyascitta* (atonement) for having done wrong to nature. They even went to the extent that in anticipation of our possibly doing any harm to nature consciously or unconsciously while getting out of the bed in the morning we were asked to beg pardon from the mother earth for touching it by feet and thereby polluting it. The sublime ideas of *sarva mangala* (universal well-being), *sarve bhavantu sukhinaḥ* (Let every one be happy), *samāja* (just corporate living), *araṇya* (a place of no-war, i.e. peaceful co-existence for different species with mutual concern in the lap of nature), *pañcavaṭi* (a place where five useful trees are grown) etc. are just to mention a few among a host of such ideas which were deeply inculcated in us. We still have their faint impressions in our mind inspite of their erosion due to the perverting influence of industrialisation and ill-conceived modernisation.[18]

The materialistic infrastructure that we have built around us through the marvels of science and technology has made us blind and indifferent to the values of matter and has misled us to forget the intimate relationship between human beings and nature. Those ideas particularly the ones which teach us to regard matter as Brahman and divinise nature should qualify us to be culturally the most advanced people in the world. That is our precious heritage which we should have tried our best to preserve, proliferate and practice. But it is both pity and irony that we people who worshipped nature and all living beings, including plants, have started ignoring them and harming them in our practical life. Instead of participating and partaking in the beauty and bounty, abundance and splendour of nature we have taken a utilitarian and exploitative attitude to it. In the past we used to follow natural principles in all our pursuits of science, technology, humanities and arts, in all modes of living and conduct. It was because of our deep commitment to nature that we were able to develop a rich, prosperous and healthy society based on equality. Following the perverted influence of the western mode of education we find that the policies and programmes adopted by us for material progress do not reflect any concern for the laws of nature or sensibility to nature. There is no awareness of the values of matter and there is lack of will for preservation of nature. We do voice our concern about the hazards of pollution but we have no will and determination to stop indiscriminate abuse, exploitation and plundering of nature. Today no one talks of spiritual bonds or spiritual unity with nature. Instead only selfish consideration and mutual accusations are expressed.

The need of the day is inculcation of nature-consciousness, care and respect of nature and eco-sensibility. Through eco-educa-tion let our children be taught to develop a healthy relationship with nature and balancing of lifestyle in accordance with the laws of nature for the establishment of a healthy, prosperous and affluent society free from hunger and disease, wants and suffering. In our educational system let us make a modest beginning at the primary school level and return to our old way of living in peace with nature.

We may conclude by pointing out to the need for radical revision of our educational curricula and syllabii and making them genuinely value-oriented. Education has to be meant for turning out true human beings. For this, we should have proper and fuller understanding of the human person. We should give up the present narrow, truncated and lopsided idea of human nature. Since the Vedic thought has quite a lot to contribute in this regard, let us revisit the Vedas without any bias and prejudice and revive and revitalise whatever is useful and valuable for our present needs and aspirations. There is nothing wrong in going back to the past with discriminative acumen, dissecting what is living and what is dead in the tradition, and reverting to that which has worth and utility.

References:

1. (i) Isa Upanisad, 11.

   (ii)Kena Upanisad, 11.12.

2. Rgveda, VII. 32.26.
3. Ibid., IV. 23.8
4. Ibid., X.90
5. Ibid., X. 13.1
6. (i) Atharva Veda, VIII.1 .6.

   (ii)Ibid., V.30.7.

7. Sa vidyā yā vimuktaye.
8. Rgveda, X. 53.6.
9. Taittirīya Upaniṣad, Ānandavalli.
10. (i) Yajurveda, XXXI. 17.

    (ii)Dhiyo yo naḥ pracodayāt. The Gayatri Mantra.

11. (i) Rgveda, X.91.2.
12. Kaṭha Upaniṣad, 1.2.1.
13. Taittirīya Upaniṣad, Bhṛguvalli, 1.6.
14. (i) Sarīramādyam khalu dharma-sādhanam. Kalidasa in Kumārasambhavam.

    (ii) Annam na nindyat.

    (iii) Aum āpyāyantu mamāngāni etc. -Kena Upanisad, Śāntipaṭha.

15. Prthivi devī namastubhyam pādasparśo kṣamasva me. -Viṣṇupurāṇa
16. Yoga Sutra, 11.32.
17. Yajurveda, 36.17.
18. (i) Mātā Bhumiḥ Putroham prthivyāḥ.

    (ii) Yo devo agnau yo apsu yo viśvam bhuvanamāviveśa.

    (iii) Yo oṣadhiṣu yo vanaspatiṣu tasmai devāya namo namaḥ.

    -Śveta. Upaniṣad

    (iv) Īśāvāsyamidam sarvam. -Īśa Upaniṣad. 1.

Buddhist Economics of Compassion and Communion

It is universally felt that all is not well with the present day thoughts and practices in the sphere of economics engulfing the entire world in a severe crisis and therefore this calls for serious thinking as to what ails the prevailing states of affair and how to rectify the root causes of the problems facing the humankind. In view of urgency of the situation apparent symptoms are to be attended and curative measures are to be adopted. But it is imperative to go to the root causes and undertake preventive and positive measures This necessitates rethinking about economic principles, policies, planning and programs.

This paper has limited concerns and stems from the disillusionment with the dichotomous, exclusivist and lopsided economic situations that obtain in the modern world and outlines a brief sketch of economic system as per the Indian Buddhist approach to structure and manage economy at the national and global levels. It is hoped that the classical Indian thought can possibly offer an effective and more beneficial alternative to the present day individualistic-materialistic-consumerist-profit seeking-competitive-exploitative economy which is bereft of welfare contents, sustainability of economic resources and spiritual orientation.

The motivating factor in presenting this paper is that if we possess something which may prove helpful and useful to world peace, progress and plenitude, we should not hesitate in sharing it with the world at large. Rather than being burden to the world or being idle spectator to the universal suffering or feeling shy in sharing cultural heritage with others, we should attempt to partake in cooperative endeavor to resolve the problems of the world and creatively reconsider what our ancient culture, civilization and traditions can contribute to the present world for a bright future, as Pandit Jawaharlal Nehru always emphasized.

There should be no denial of the fact that the inquisitive mind is looking for a redeeming knowledge. The western economic thought seems to have reached a point of saturation resulting in a global economic turmoil. Therefore it calls for a bold initiative for paradigm shift for which some directions can come from the classical Buddhist thought. The Buddhist approach is that of a moderate economy based on 'Buddhist Middle Path' which is sustainable both in production and consumption that are the two aspects of economic planning and development. The Buddhist way is an economy of balanced development, balancing different pairs like production and consumption, individual and society, nation and universe, physical and spiritual, present and future and so forth. It is holistic and integral approach to economic issues from micro and macro perspectives, which measures development in terms of prosperity, health and happiness of the present and the future generations in terms of intra-generational and inter-generational justice. It provides for a cosmos-friendly economy in which instrumental and intrinsic goods are put in a symmetrical and balanced harmony. It is an economy of compassion and communion, of peace and non-violence. Full details can be worked out on the basis of the seminal ideas presented here, as only a blueprint is provided at this juncture for perusal of concerned and interested scholars.

Buddhism is both a view of reality and a way of life seeking to realize the *summum bonum* of existence. It has therefore an all comprehensive perspective on all facets of reality and life. Its understanding of economic aspect of our life has something fresh, unique and of great contemporary relevance and may serve the need for a desirable alternative model at the national and global levels. It attends to all the four drivers of economic development, viz., human resources, natural resources, capital resources and innovative technology. Though it has not been presented very systematically in the classical Buddhist literature, it can be reconstructed from the discourses of the Buddha with rulers of his times contained in the early Buddhist literature supplementing this with other classical literature and given a coherent shape. Buddhist Economy is based on and can be derived from the teachings of Lord Buddha in the well known *Dhammacakkapavattanasutta* in which the 'Four Noble Truths' and the 'Eight-fold Noble Path' contained in them are propagated. But in the Pali texts we get sufficient material for constructing an economic theory.

Buddhist Economy is essentially characterized by love and compassion, benevolence and altruism, interdependence and interrelation, mutual openness and reciprocity, fellowship and participation, plenitude and happiness, giving and renouncing, caring and sharing. The four noble virtues for ideal human conduct named as *Brahmaviharas* (global virtues) of universal friendship and amity (*maitta*), universal compassion (*karuna*), universal responsibility making others happy (*mudita*) and indifference to narrow self-interest (*upeksha*) are the guiding principles on which economic thought and planning and economic behavior of individual and society are to be based. It is an integral and organic approach which is holistic and non-divisive and takes into its purview well being of the entire cosmos (*lokanukampaya*). Morality and universal responsibility are the very heart of Buddhism and therefore

Buddhist economics is dharmic (ethical) being guided by virtuous mind (*kusala citta*). It can be described as **dharma-oriented** and **dharma-based** economy. Its motto is morality first, money thereafter. Morality is not a policy but a principle of life and existence. There are three facets of dharma; it is sustaining, it is regulating and it is instrumental for good. *Prajna* (wisdom) and *Sila* (morality) as *karuna* (compassion) are the two foundations on which it rests. Economics like other human pursuits are only the means and its ultimate goal is cosmic well-being and happiness (*bahujana hitaya, bahujana sukhaya*) leading to realization of *summum bonum* of life (*nirvana*).

One of the most significant implications of the Buddhist non-substantiality view (*Anatmavada*) of Reality is that the cosmos, rather the cosmic process, is a totality of fleeting occurrences and not of things. It is a highly complex, complicated and intricate but planned and purposive networking of events and not a mechanistic arrangement of preexistent entities. Every worldly existence has a dependent origination out of a causal collocation characterized by mutuality and openness, interrelatedness and reciprocity. Each one depending upon ones nature has a specific nature, place, role and function in the cosmic setup as determined in the scheme of the universe. Human existence is not in isolation with the rest of the universe. It is not in the form of just "I' but also 'we'. In the economic functioning every one has to contribute according to ones ability. The cosmos is a network of relationship of interdependence giving rise to organic collective living (*samgha jivana*) like that of an organism. As Hua-yen Buddhism puts it,

In one is all, in many is one

One is identical to all, many is identical to one.

The natural implications of such a view point are non-individualism, non-isolationism, non-selfishness etc. in negative terms and mutual dependence, collective living and corporate functioning in positive language. The model of a living organism is best suited to explain this position. A living organism is a dynamic totality of multiple organs at once holistic and integral, centrifugal and centripetal, collective and individual. Here whole lives for the parts and parts live for the whole. There is mutuality and reciprocity in a natural way, a sort of pre-established harmony. Every one discharges ones duties and obligations without caring for ones rights. It is duty-oriented rather than rights-oriented. There is coordination and cooperation which is generally smooth and if it gets disturbed the result is sickness and ailment and possible decay. The ideal requirement is maintenance of harmony. Harmony is natural and to be preserved, and imbalance is unnatural, to be avoided. This organic approach which is holistic and integral has some elements of 'panpsychism'.

The basic concepts underlying the Buddhist approach to economics are middle path (*madhyama marga*), right living (*samyag ajivaka*), collective living (*samgha Jivana*), interdependence and interrelation of all phenomena (*pratitya samutpada*), preservation, conservation and consolidation of all resources (*ksema*), enhancement and revitalization of all existing resources (*yoga*), non-profiteering and non-deprivation of others ensuring intra-generational justice (*asteya*), safeguarding and preserving the resources for the posterities as intergenerational justice (*aparigraha*), management of end, means and modalities in a planned, purposive and efficacious manner (*upaya kausala*), and self-reliance (*purusartha*). In his discourses on economic issues, on agriculture, trade, commerce and industry, on business enterprises, on monetary transactions and the like Buddha has expounded these ideas very clearly and the *Tripitakas* (Buddhist sacred literature) are replete with them. Sometimes he explains them directly, and sometimes through stories and parables.

The non-substantial approach has deep and tremendous impact in shaping the Buddhist economy. Since it advocates egoless-ness it avoids individualism and all its corollaries. No individual is isolated existence. Every individual depends on the other. There is supportive mutualism. Individual-centeredness degenerates into narrow individualism which breeds all sorts of economic offences, conflicts and deprivations. It leads to consumerism and profiteering, unlawful practices and alienation. Buddhist economy respects individual and individual freedom, personal initiative, preferences, choices and actions but also calls for universal responsibilities. It believes that pursuit of individualistic goods at the cost of others is counterproductive in the ultimate analysis. Since every existence is interdependent and interrelated Buddhism advocates holistic and integral understanding of the nature of reality in general and of economic reality in particular. It is feeling of oneness and selfsameness with all. This is the meaning of spirituality in Indian context. Santideva in *Bodhicaryavatara*, eighth chapter, uses two poignant words *paratmasamata* (feeling of selfsameness with others) and *paratmaparivartana* (transforming oneself as others, a sort of empathy) for this. This also finds expression in the famous four *Brahmaviharas* of *Maitri* (fellowship), *Karuna* (compassion), *Mudita* (rejoicing at the happiness of others) and *Upeksa* (indifference to self-interest) referred to earlier.

Buddhist economy is based on the doctrine of middle path avoiding the extremes of materialism and idealism, capitalism and communism, individualism and totalitarianism, poverty and affluence, self-negation and self-indulgence. It ensures consumption without consumerism. It accepts profit without profiteering. Profit is not to be used solely for personal purposes. It is to be utilized for growth and development, for helping the needy and for benevolent purposes like education. Buddhist economy emphasizes social component with the ultimate goal of cosmic well-being. As Lord Buddha exhorted his disciples, "O Monks! Move around for the well-being of every one, for the happiness of every one, showering compassion on the entire world; for the good, for the welfare of divine and human." (*Vinaya Pitaka* I.23)

In the present day economic mode people are first induced to desire and use things which are produced or to be produced. This is consumerism. In consumerism demand follows production. More and more consumption is sought through inducements of various types so that sales increase and profit accrues. Whatever is produced must be sold and consumed and profit generated. As far as possible disposable goods should be produced so that they can soon be discarded and newer production may be facilitated. Newer demands are created by producing more attractive and enticing goods. This also leads to competition among the producers and sellers. The entire management of economic planning, production and distribution is geared towards this goal. Those who can help in doing so are termed as 'management gurus'. In the Buddhist system the scenario should be just the opposite. Human being is not born to consume whatever is produced. Production is for human being and human being is not for production. Production should be only for meeting the demands and as far as possible demands are to be curbed and not increased. Since production follows demand and since demands should be reduced to minimum, production has to be need-based. Any sort of cross materialism is not in keeping with Buddhist view point. Economic enterprise is only to meet the legitimate needs and necessities, and not to cater to greed. Thus, in contrast to the individualistic-consumerist, profit-oriented economy of the present times based on the culture of 'having', of acquisition and possession, of extravagant consumption and excessive indulgence, Buddhism offers an alternative model of the culture of 'giving', of sacrifice, of renunciation, of peace, harmony and cooperation, of lawfulness and of respect to environment. It calls for fulfillment of needs but not to cater to greed. It repudiates competitive economy and calls for cooperative economy. The Buddhist economy can therefore offer a new approach, fresh insights, deeper intuitions and a new rationality for a paradigm shift, a shift which is natural as human fulfillment lies only in the alternative set of values. In this shift the focal point of economy is not profit but service, not exploitation but judicious employment of resources. Digganikaya (III.p.168) gives the example of a bee which gathers honey without damaging flower and spares honey for consumptions by others. This cares for ecological purity and balance, justice and fair play. It is conducive to holistic growth, human and cosmic.

The culture of 'giving' is not motivated by selfish considerations of getting name and fame, or power and prestige. Greatness of a person depends not in amassing wealth or in showing it off for charity. It depends on character of benevolence. It is not ego-satisfaction or for seeking return-favors. It is for cosmic well-being (*bahujanahitaya*). It is selfless giving. It is giving for social and cosmic peace, prosperity and plenitude. It is giving with joy and for joy. It is sharing of material and spiritual goods. It is an economy in which need of everyone is taken care of but greed of none is catered to. It is not an economy of extravagance, spendthrift-ness and wastefulness. This calls for the role of *wisdom* and *compassion* in economics. In a discourse with king Pasenadi in the *Suttanipata* Buddha tells him that a person who acquires wealth and does not use it for the wellbeing of himself and others is not praiseworthy.

Buddhism recognizes importance of wealth for happy and contended worldly life. In Buddhist economy wealth is a means and not an end. The means must be pure and conducive to end which also has to be pure. This is *samyak ajivaka*. The end is not hedonistic pleasure but moral and spiritual uplift. Wealth is neither an evil nor it is a final end. It is to be acquired in a *dharmic* (pious and righteous) way, with legitimate limits and restraints. This is known as *utthanasampada*. In the *Andhasutta* of *Anguttaranikaya* Buddha says that a person who is poverty stricken is like a blind. One who tries to acquire wealth but does not care about the righteousness of means of acquisition is like one-eyed person. The two-eye person is one who distinguishes between good and bad. Ethical and spiritual orientation is the key note of Buddhist economy. Wealth and virtue should go hand in hand. Buddhism calls for balancing of wants and consumption, of labour and leisure, of income and expenditure. This moderation is technically known as *samajivita*. (*Anguttaranikaya*, IV. P.281). This balancing is possible by cultivation of *apramada* (vigilant attitude). In following the middle path there should be neither poverty nor affluence, neither austerity nor excessive indulgence. Life should be neither stringent nor extravagant. There shculd be neither misuse of wealth nor enslavement to wealth. One should not feel elated when wealth comes nor should one be miserable and depressed when wealth departs. This sort of indifference is best suited to mental peace. The attainment of given end with minimum means is *upayakausala* (skillful employment of means). It is a symbiosis of end, means and modalities. It is maximum output with minimum input, maximum realization with minimum possession and consumption. Buddhism recons with 'will to exist', and 'to exist in a moderately good way' ensuring quality of life. Buddhist economy cares for quality of life and good standard of living but this is to be measured qualitatively and not quantitatively. Moreover, Buddhist economy is economy of non-violence, non-violence to ones own self, non-violence to others and to the total cosmos. For Buddhist way of life economic behavior is purposeful in gathering tangible wealth for balanced material consumption and for accumulating merits for future life. It provides a basis to worldly life and also to moral and spiritual life. Buddha realized the need and importance of wealth. With empty stomach one can not get wisdom nor can one teach wisdom. Buddha, therefore, did not preach to hungry persons. With poverty all evils come, economic offences are generated and social institutions are disrupted and destroyed. With economic growth social order and peace are established. It is advocacy of mixed economy with individual initiative and state control. This message is clearly conveyed in the *Cakkvatthisimhanadasutta* and *Katadantasutta*.

Buddhist economy has both micro and macro dimensions. It attends to all facets of economy agriculture, industry, trade and commerce, business and fiscal policies. It deals with employment, production, distribution, consumption and development of economy. It explicitly states what is to be produced, how to be produced, how much is to be produced and for whom it is to be produced. The same applies to consumption as well. Economy is to be evaluated depending upon the way it is produced and consumed. Care is to taken that there is no violence or harm to self and to other living beings and to nature. As stated earlier, non-violence is at the center stage of Buddhist economy. The doctrine of karma comes as a guiding principle in structuring the economic system in so far as it emphasizes rational action and intentionality coupled with universal responsibility. One must possess *pious mind* for righteous livelihood.

Humane development is the keynote of Buddhist Economy. Development is for human being and not that human being is for development. But it is sustainable development of the entire cosmos and not just human development. It involves seven factors, viz., human agency, human motivation, material resources, monetary system, technological support, management at different levels, and market for distribution. The development and management of economy in the Buddhist framework touches all the three phases of production, distribution and consumption keeping in view the law of demand and supply. The motivating factor is not first production and then creation of demand; rather it stands for production only for satisfaction of legitimate demand. Economic planning comes under *Upaya kausal* (skillful and efficacious employment of means). It has two stages. One is management of action and the other is management of the results of action. It is emphasized that we must know what is to act, why to act, and how to act. We must act in most skillful manner so as to realize the desired result. Management of result is to be guided by intra-generational and intergenerational justice. Our wants are unlimited but resources are limited and exhaustible though renewable to some extent. Our wants are increasing day by day; our desires remain in-satiated. Consumerism has led to more and more hankering after sensuous pleasures and desire for fulfillment of carnal appetites. Strictly speaking our needs are limited but wants are becoming unlimited. So we have to set limits to our wants and cease to be 'ever-wanting storehouse'. We wrongly think that nature has infinite resources or that all resources should be geared for our benefits only. According to Buddha the problem of scarcity leads to unjust distribution and consequent poverty. Wealth can generate resources but cannot remove scarcity. So we have to control our wants and desires (*tanha*) making a distinction between need and greed.

Buddhism as a school of thought and a way of life is at once both ancient and modern. It proved useful in the past and could spread all over Asia, not by force but by conviction and usefulness. In modern times also it has attracted the minds of the elites all over the world. But ramifications of its seminal ideas are yet to be worked out in different fields of human and cosmic life as per the modern needs and aspirations. Buddha was a practical and pragmatic person and he had genuine concern for human and cosmic wellbeing. It is high time that Buddha's teachings are made to out step the confinements of religious or academic enterprises, though they are also useful, and other dimensions are also attended to. It is revisiting Buddhism with fresh insights and innovative ideas and creative reinterpretations. Perhaps a collective thinking and multidisciplinary team work may be more helpful. It is hoped that the Buddhist alternative will be reconstructed and given a fair trial to ameliorate the human miseries, as was the objective of the Buddha.

The paper is published in "***Prajna Vihara***", **Assumption University of Thailand, Bangkok**, Vol.9, No.1, January-June, 2008